Nebula Maker
&
Four Encounters

Nebula Maker
&
Four Encounters

by Olaf Stapledon

with illustrations by
Jim Starlin

DODD, MEAD & COMPANY
New York

First published in the United States in 1983

1 2 3 4 5 6 7 8 9 10

Library of Congress Cataloging in Publication Data

Stapledon, Olaf, 1886-1950.
  Nebula maker; & Four encounters.

  1. Science fiction, English. I. Stapledon, Olaf,
1886-1950. Four encounters. 1983. II. Title.
III. Title: Nebula maker; and, Four encounters.
PR6037.T18A6   1983   823'.912   82-17684
ISBN 0-396-08105-3 (hardcover)
ISBN 0-396-08167-3 (paperback)

Contents

Illustrations

Introduction

Though more than fifty years have passed, I can still visualize the very shelf (it was just below knee level) in the Minehead Public Library where I discovered *Last and First Men*. No other book had a greater influence on my life.

Olaf Stapledon's most famous work was published in 1930, to considerable applause from a wide range of reviewers. "As original as the solar system," said Hugh Walpole, while Arnold Bennett commended the author's "tremendous and beautiful imagination." It was also praised by a failed politician, now earning a living by his pen—one Winston S. Churchill. Almost at once it became one of those works that define a genre—which is somewhat ironic in view of the fact that Stapledon had never even heard of "science fiction" when he was writing his "story of the near and far future."

Last and First Men and its successor, *Star Maker* (1937), are the twin summits of a literary career that began just before World War I, ended soon after World War II, and was profoundly influenced by both conflicts. One touching proof of that lies on my desk at this moment.

It is with an awe approaching reverence that I now hold in my hands the slim volume *Latter-Day Psalms* (Liverpool: Henry Young & Sons, Ltd., 1914) and read the inscription "Miss H. M. Barnard, with the author's compliments. Christmas 1914." Tucked inside is a letter to the recipient, on a single folded sheet with the embossed heading "Annery, Caldy, West Kirby (Telephone 215 Hoylake)." It is written in a copper plate, which later became the most minute but legible script I have ever encountered, and is dated 22 December 1914—four months after the guns of August started to thunder across Europe.

"My dear Miss Barnard," it begins. "Will you please accept the enclosed small token of affection and respect, with best wishes for Christmas and the New Year. Let us hope for peace before the close of 1915. . . ."

This first book by "Wm. Olaf Stapledon," as he signs himself (though the *W* is omitted on the title page), was what would now be called a vanity edition. "Father has got it published for me, which is very good of him, as of course I could not have financed it." This admission of dependency seems a little surprising for a man who was, after all, past his twenty-eighth birthday.

The letter continues with an intriguing remark: "I am in the midst of another and larger effort, but the war distracts one; and anyhow I cannot get it done before April, when at latest I am going to take a commission." I wonder what that "effort" could have been; Stapledon's next book, *A Modern Theory of Ethics,* did not appear for another fifteen years.

Miss Barnard was apparently a Quaker, because

the letter expresses the view that the war "must be terrible for such fervent peace-lovers as the Friends. I think I shall be as fervent before I have done." This proved to be the case; Stapledon spent three years with the Friends' Ambulance Unit.

The rest of the short letter concerns family matters and contains a wistful reference to "the girls from Adelaide." (Soon after the war, Stapledon married an Australian girl, Agnes Miller.) "I am longing for news. Yet I have no desire to see my cousin again till I have had my share of the war. Then we will begin a new age."

A new age was indeed beginning, though it was hardly an improvement on the old one. And yet another was starting when an older and sadder Stapledon wrote *Four Encounters,* which can be dated to late 1945 or early 1946 by its reference to the atomic bomb and "prisoners of war, demolishing an old air-raid shelter."

Stapledon was probably still working on *Four Encounters* when I had my only personal encounter with him, in 1948. The British Interplanetary Society had invited him to London to give a talk, "Interplanetary Man" *(J.B.I.S.,* November 1948; reprinted in *The Coming of the Space Age,* New York: Meredith Press, and London: Gollancz, 1967). With shame and incredulity I confess that I recall nothing of that meeting—even though I opened the discussion and had dinner with our speaker after his talk.

But I do remember the impact of Stapledon's personality; the two words that always come to mind when I think of him are *gentleness* and *nobility.* Though he has always had many devoted followers, in his own time and for thirty years after his death he was shamefully neglected—and even misrepresented. Now he speaks to us more clearly than he could ever address his contemporaries.

They cannot be blamed for their failure to share his vision; the space age had to dawn before the world could understand Stapledon's thoughts and look through his eyes. It is sad that he died too soon to see the first journeys beyond the atmosphere; had he lived as long as H. G. Wells (who, aged eighty, predeceased him by only four years), he would have witnessed the birth of Apollo.

I do not know if Wells and Stapledon ever met in the flesh, but they certainly did in spirit. So it seems appropriate to end this tribute to Stapledon with his great precursor's most famous words, which surely express the hopes and fears of both men:

For Mankind it is the Universe—or nothing.
Which shall it be?

ARTHUR C. CLARKE
Colombo, Sri Lanka
14 May 1982

Nebula Maker

Contents

Synopsis of the Book

Contents page from the first draft of *Star Maker*

Introduction
to the British Edition

1

Nebula Maker represents the earliest record we have of the original concepts and plans that Olaf Stapledon made for *Star Maker*. The "Synopsis of the Book" indicates that the original plan of the work was "linear," starting with the creation of our universe and proceeding to the age of the nebulae, the age of the stars, and on to life on planetary systems. As eventually published, the organization was drastically altered, and the origin of our universe was relegated to a position near the end of the work, the end and beginning of the universe being considered in the same chapter.

Examination of the Synopsis also indicates that many of the first chapters of *Star Maker* were entirely absent from the early plan and were evidently added at a later stage of the work's development. Other differences are apparent in the concept of the work, particularly in the personalities of the narrator and the nebulae themselves. The narrator of *Star Maker* represents in microcosm a part of that "community" toward which all the intelligences of the

5

universes of Stapledon strive. The narrator of *Nebula Maker* displays awe and disbelief as his major characteristics, and all traces of communal feeling are absent. This early narrator is rather more impersonal and distant than the narrator of the work published in 1937. A visitor to West Kirby, Cheshire, England, can still almost recognize the town as described in the first and last sections of the book. However, the suburb pictured in the original concept is rather abstract and diffuse. Stapledon added to the dimensions of the final plan by including himself in the work as narrator and inserting references which can be recognized as personal statements.

The personalities of the nebulae were altered in the opposite fashion from the early to the late design of the work. The initial concept describes creatures with a rich artistic and historical heritage; the final concept pictures rather simpler primitive creatures almost unable to communicate with one another, and having no history.

The questions naturally arise, why this change in the characteristics of the nebulae, and why was the detailed historical description of these hugest of creatures entirely removed from *Star Maker?* Several answers suggest themselves. By abstracting the personalities of the creatures Stapledon succeeds in making them appear stranger and more remote than could any detailed description, and the change in concept of the work required that many more recognizably "human" societies be pictured, societies with which a human reader can more easily identify. In addition, by creating a detailed history for these creatures, Stapledon originally made them appear almost human and accessible, a concept which he eventually abandoned. However, he did make use of some of the physical descriptions in the final plan.

2

Nebula Maker describes in great detail the evolutionary history of the nebulae and, as such, is a major contribution to the works of Olaf Stapledon. Here he has depicted a society of intelligent beings whose psychology and aesthetics are completely different from any group of creatures described in his other works of fiction, and, indeed, in any other works of science fiction. The nebulae are devoid of senses familiar to human beings, suffer under no economic constraints, and have not been shaped by evolutionary pressures. Their modes of perception and psychology are remote from ours, yet they are described with such care and fidelity to detail that they achieve a poignant reality, a reality which allows the author to delineate the relationships among these creatures and to create a history which is a rational unfolding of the consequences of that psychology and sense of aesthetics.

Stapledon previously attempted to portray a society of such strangeness and remoteness in the chapters in *Last and First Men* which deal with the Martian intelligences. The nebulae, however, despite their utter dissimilarity to humanity, retain a close link to humanity because they are individuals rather than "swarm" creatures, as were the Martians. Because the nebulae are individuals, Stapledon has been able to create two personalities which achieve the reality and mythic power of many of his other characters. These personalities are Bright Heart and Fire Bolt. They represent, respectively, aspects of human personality Stapledon considered to be the most significant in human history, the Saint and the Revolutionary. In this work the relationships of these personality types to society and to each other is described, and the consequences of their acts determine nebular history.

3

Many of the problems which Stapledon considered to be of greatest importance are here treated, but, of course, they are refracted through the aesthetic sensibilities and psychology of the nebulae. The relationships of the individual to society, the results of industrialism and progress, the necessity for artistic creation, the desire to manipulate and dominate—all are considered here, as they were considered in *Last and First Men, Odd John, Star Maker,* and *Darkness and the Light.* The need for balance, and the difficulty with which that balance is achieved, are depicted in *Nebula Maker* as clearly as they are in those earlier works.

Although *Nebula Maker,* obviously, comprises only one-quarter of the total plan of the early version of *Star Maker,* it does stand as a major creative achievement of its author. We may speculate about the remainder of the early manuscript. Perhaps those unfound portions were never written, perhaps they were incorporated into the final version of the book, or perhaps they were considered to be of inferior quality by the author and were ultimately destroyed. Whatever the fate of that part of the manuscript, we are most fortunate that Stapledon did save the portion we now call *Nebula Maker*.

Harvey Satty
Chairman, The Olaf Stapledon Society

1. Starlight on a Hill

I have seen God creating the cosmos, watching its growth, and finally destroying it.

Call me, if you will, a liar or a madman. Say I lack humor, say that my claim is sacrilegious and in the worst taste. Yet I have indeed seen God. I have seen him creating, watching, destroying.

I tell myself that I must have been affected not through the bodily eye but through the eye of the mind, that the whole experience must have flooded up within me from the hidden springs of my own imagination. But whether the teeming and fantastic events that I have witnessed were revealed by external or by internal vision, revealed they surely were. I did not construct them. They thrust themselves upon me, compelling belief.

Others have no reason to share my conviction. Therefore simply as a story I set down the record of my hypercosmical experience, confidant that, if I can present it clearly, it must by its sheer strangeness and majesty compel at least attention, if not belief.

But can human language convey even a thousandth part of the wonders that I still so vividly

11

remember? They unfolded themselves before me with all the forcefulness and detail of perceived reality. But how can I describe them? Here is the white page, and there "in my mind" the crowded and overburdened memory of aeons past and future, and of time systems wholly distinct from ours. By what magic can I so guide my pen that from its gray trail, and from the printed pages which its course will determine, some glimmer, some pale distorted reflection, of my experience may be projected into other minds?

The vision occurred about two hours after midnight. I cannot bring myself to describe the torturing personal contact that had befallen me earlier in the night. I will say only that it had filled me with an overwhelming, a blinding sense of the beauty and the precariousness of human personality, and indeed of one person, in whom, as it then seemed to me, all sweetness and all bitterness were together embodied. So complete was my preoccupation that I had lost sight, so to speak, of the universe. I could no longer rise above my own misery by reminding myself that personal calamity, even the complete ruin of many fair personal spirits, is demanded for the wholeness and beauty of the cosmos.

When I had left the mean little villa and the presence of the being that had so moved me, I must have hurried along the empty streets in complete abstraction, with my mind nailed still to the immediate past; for suddenly I found myself sitting on the heathery top of the hill which overlooks the suburb and the sea. I found also that I was weeping. This was a novel experience.

Whether in self-pity or self-mockery, I performed the gesture that millions of my fellow mortals must have carried out in faith and hope. I looked up to heaven.

The stars glittered with a brilliance and profusion rare in England. The Milky Way, a vague and feathery stream, phosphorescent, pricked with diamonds, divided the heavens. I was infuriated, and then utterly cowed, by the insensitiveness and vastness of the cosmos. By what right, by what right could these mindless gulfs drown the personal loveliness that had become all in all to me?

Still gazing upward, I noticed something in the darkness between the stars. At first it seemed no more than the vague shifting illumination which the eye discovers in itself when robbed of external light. But now, to my amazement, to my bewilderment and horror, but also to my incredulous amusement, I recognized that an immense and dimly lucent face was regarding me from behind the stars, from behind the Milky Way.

The fearsome thing was spread over half the sky. And it was upside down. The eyes were low in the south. The chin mounted to the zenith and beyond. Down toward the northern horizon loomed titanic shoulders, and far below them a confusion of many arms.

Such a vision clearly meant madness. It was impossible that there should be anything of the nature of a human or half-human form behind the galaxy, peering through a veil of stars. The apparition, taken at its face value, violated the whole teaching of modern science.

I know not whether I was more distressed at my derangement, or shocked at the devastatingly bad taste of the hallucination which confronted me, or tickled by the thought of the discomfiture which our scientists would suffer were it after all proved a true perception.

Anxiety for my own sanity forced me to take firm hold on myself. Derisively I reflected that this was too crude, too banal an illusion for a scientifically minded person like me. Maidservants or savages might be haunted by such a phantom; but I, with my skeptical intelligence, could surely dismiss it by merely ridiculing it. Still gazing skyward, I recalled to mind the empty vastness of transgalactic space. But the image remained in view, and grew clearer.

Panic threatened me; but with a desperate effort I thrust it back. In order to calm myself, I undertook a careful study of the apparition, which indeed was so novel that even the dread of insanity could not wholly quench my curiosity.

So as to see it in the normal position, I lay flat on the heather with my head thrown back. The celestial face was like no other face, or like all faces. It was human, yet not human, animal, yet not animal, divine, yet surely not divine. I was subtly reminded of the grotesque gods of Egypt and of India, and also of the mild enigmatic expression of certain African carvings. I found myself thinking both of beasts of rapine and of gentler beasts. I saw expressions not only of tiger, hawk and snake, but also of ox and deer, elephant and gentle ape. But in the visage which overhung me, these characters, though seemingly alien to one another, were so subtly blended that they presented not a composite form made up of features selected from all living things, but one archetypal unity, from which the terrestrial creatures might well have borrowed each its distinctive nature.

The longer I regarded it, the more the apparition mastered me. It compelled me into an amazed, reluctant admiration. To call it merely beautiful would be to malign it. It was ugly, damnably ugly, almost satanic. Its anthropomorphism, hideously mixed with sheer animality, violated the austere inhumanity of the night sky. Yet in its own unique manner it was mysteriously, piercingly beautiful. It gave me a strange sense that hitherto, all my life long, I had looked in the wrong direction for the most excellent of all kinds of beauty. It outraged me as some new mode in music or sculpture may at once outrage and revitalize the mind. Its significance tantalized and escaped me. The celestial eyes gazed at me, or gazed seemingly at me, from under the bright brow so darkly that they seemed to express equally a Buddhalike serenity, a brute's indifference, and a rapier alertness.

Presently the apparition was transformed. I discovered that it was no single constant face but a succession of face forms imperceptibly changing into one another. It was as though the flux of thought in this being so remodeled the whole structure of its visage that nothing was left the same but a subtle air of personal continuity and identity. As a cloud changes from shape to shape, so this phantom suffered a continuous metamorphosis in such a manner that I saw it now as a mythical beast, now as a fair young man with battle in his nostrils, now as a sphinx, now as a mother bowed over her child, now as the child crucified, now as a jesting fiend, now as a huge inhuman insect face with many-faceted eyes and pincer-mandibles, now for a fleeting moment as the white-bearded Jehovah.

Yet, mysteriously, I continued to feel through all these transformations the presence of the one unique and superb personality which had at the outset confronted me.

The transformations became more rapid, more bewildering. The features disintegrated from one another. Instead of a face there were a thousand eyes intermingled with a thousand searching or constructing hands. I seemed to detect also, in the obscure depths of the vision, a thousand phallic shapes, flaccid, rampant.

Yet even through these many and fantastic changes I retained the sense that I was beholding no mere chaos of images but manifestations of the unique, the superb one.

"It is God, it is God," I said to myself. But I knew that if indeed there is a God he is no more visible than the theory of relativity. With ever lessening conviction, I reminded myself that I was mad. Even so it was impossible to believe that so novel, so overmastering an apparition was nothing whatever but a figment of insanity.

"It is indeed God," I affirmed to myself. "It is God stirring my mad mind to create true though fantastic symbols of himself." So at least I comforted myself.

By now I had lost sight of the stars. I had lost all

perception of the planet to which I was clinging. Even my own body seemed to have melted and vanished. Yet inwardly my mind was clear, and indeed quickened to an unaccustomed agility. I remembered minutely the sequence of events that had led me to this vision. I remembered the whole trend of my life, with its many groping and unfulfilled activities. I remembered the contemporary world crisis in human affairs, the millions of unemployed, the recrudescence of barbarism in Europe and America, the forlorn struggle for a new world.

Under the innumerable and cryptic eyes of God I found myself searching in all these terrestrial aspects for some new significance. But I could not seize it.

2. Creation

A startling change now took place in my mind. My reverie was shattered as a dream at the moment of waking, and I became aware that I had long been observing a vast pattern of cosmical and hypercosmical events. I remembered that I had been watching the visible apparition of God not for moments but for aeons, and that I had seen him create cosmos after cosmos. Now at last I was to behold God's latest creation. I was to attend the birth of that intricate and tragic cosmos, fashioned of nebulae and stars, in which mankind occurs. Would this, his latest, be also his final sketch, before he should venture on some more finished work, which perhaps would raise his spirit from time into eternity, from mere progress to perfection?

Out of the confusion of limbs and organs which had confronted me, a face now formed itself, displaying its profile. Recognizably it was the face of God, the unique one; but this was not the God of the Jews nor of the Christians, nor was it Zeus nor Allah, nor any other deity of men. It was feline, snakelike. It was lean and keen and ruthless.

Horror seized me. Could this, this living poleax, be the face of the true God? Could the spirit that this thing expressed be the one reality behind men's dreams, the dreams that they had reverently perfected through the ages? Where was the Love, and where the Wisdom; where even the Justice and the Righteousness?

In a mean suburb of a dark commercial city, had I not known a woman? Was she not fair though marred, gentle, though turning to bitterness? Surely in her there was more divinity than in this deity.

Yet as I watched I was compelled to worship.

Beneath God's face the innumerable, shadowy, restless creative hands aimlessly fingered the pale glimmer which I knew was chaos, the formless potentiality of matter, the sleeping potentiality of mind.

It seemed that in the dark spirit which is God there was not peace but restlessness, and the insistent need to create.

But presently I observed in God's eyes, God's serpent eyes, a sudden intentness; as though, peering into the jungle of his own nature he had glimpsed some new, some exquisite idea.

And now I seemed to discover in my memory that though God had triumphed in each of his many created universes, yet he had every time destroyed what he had made. Always there had come a stage in the growth of his creature, when though perfectly fulfilling his plan, it had also stung him into new percipience, and into vague new desire beyond the capacity of the poor creature to satisfy. And so, time and again God had reduced his cosmos to chaos, either with one swift, tender-contemptuous stroke of his almightiness, or slowly, delighting to observe its cycle completed by long drawn out senescence and death.

A full light, a full intelligence, now gleamed in the eyes of God. The quarry was now clearly visible, the new conception apprehended. Looking down once more upon his chaos, God now took purposeful hold of it with all the sinewy cooperative gangs of his hands.

He drew out from chaos a minute portion, so minute that it lay on the point of his finger as a mote upon a continent.

Earnestly for a while God gazed upon this infinitesimal, considering how to work his will upon it. Then delicately he rolled it between a finger and a thumb, vitalizing it with the novel urge of his conception. But he sealed its potencies within it, so that for the present it should express nothing of its nature. Yet to my divinely stimulated vision it appeared as a very minute dark pearl, dimly shining by the reflected light of God's own person.

Earnestly God regarded his little creature. And he saw that it was indeed made according to his plan, that he had indeed with agile fingers fashioned it to be the bearer of lofty and diverse potentialities; so that, when he should see fit to unseal its energies, it might be the vehicle both of physical power and of mentality, that it might play a part equally well in the interior of a star or in the brain of a man, and equally in the life of a saint or of a blackguard.

And now God set about to pass the whole of chaos

between his fingertips. As flax issuing from between the fingers of a woman spinning, comes forth as thread, so from God's countless fingers chaos issued as fine threads of smoke.

As the ultimate electric and vital units came into being, God counted them. Soon there were as many of them as would go to the making of a spermato- zoon, and soon as many as would be contained in a sun. And presently there was so much of the tenuous and granular substance of the cosmos as might form the warp and weft of a million galaxies. But God did not stay until he had used up all chaos, and the number of the beings which he had made was the number which his conception demanded, even to the last unit.

The host of the units was an obscurity floating around the hands and arms of God, and over his thighs and genitals, and above his head.

With all his hands, God now took hold of sleeping matter and gathered it in as a seaman a bellying sail. He furled it in upon itself. And in so doing he geometrized it according to his conception. Search- ingly he threaded his new-made matter through and through with the tracks of his ubiquitous and corre- lating fingers; so that, when he should give the word, the potencies of the cosmos should issue orderly.

Then God withdrew his hands from the entrails of his creature. And his many hands poised lovingly over it and around it and under it.

And now, looking once more at God's face, I saw that it was kindled, enspirited with expectation of the beauty and the horror which were to come.

The slumbering cosmos appeared to me now as a

smooth orb of darkness. For all its energies were still sealed within its unit members. The black sphere of the cosmos shimmered between God's hands like a huge inky bubble. Its surface reflected to me a dim and contracted image of his hands and of his lucent face.

It seemed to me that creation was now completed, and that God's new cosmos was ready to set out upon its long adventure. But I was mistaken.

For now with sudden violence God pressed upon his creature with all his hands and from every side, so that the tenuous dark orb was crushed together, and the myriad floating units were crowded ever closer and closer.

And God constricted the cosmos until every unit coincided with every other, and the cosmos was no larger than any single one of them. It now lay upon the fingertip of God, and the rest of his hands were drawn away from it.

Within the atom-cosmos were all the potencies for many million galaxies, and for storied worlds innumerable. Yet the pregnant members of the cosmos, though coincident each with all, remained inert to one another. For God had not yet broken the seals that he had set on them.

God gazed long upon his creature. And he smiled. And all his hands were still.

Then God spoke to the dark and slumbering germ of the cosmos. And he said, "Let there be light."

Immediately the seals were broken that God had set upon the myriad primal members of the cosmos. And the cosmic germ burst into life.

3. The Cosmos Is Launched

A dazzling, an unsupportable brilliance leapt at me and engulfed me. Around, above, below was light fiercer than the sun's disc at noon. Light stabbed me through and through from every side with its innumerable incandescent blades.

I had a strange sense that these transfixing blades were the stings of live things, or the claws of some great beast that had burst its fetters and now ranged free. This conviction my reason firmly rejected, but in vain. I could not but believe that the myriad primal members of the cosmos were now at last willfully putting forth their strength against one another in furious glee. Clearly they had extricated themselves from one another so violently that the atom-cosmos had exploded and become a firmament of light.

Presently I noticed a very distressing conflict in my experience. Though I was immersed in the cosmical explosion, I continued nevertheless all the while to see the cosmos as a minute and gloomy pearl quiescent on God's finger. All the while it reflected in miniature the hands and intent eyes of God.

At first I was stunned by the disaccord of these experiences, but presently I understood what had happened.

In answer to God's command, the atom-cosmos had burgeoned not only with light but with a space and time peculiar to itself. And I, by some means or other, had gained a footing therein; but without ceasing to participate in the space and time peculiar to God.

Thus, so long as I gazed at the dark seed-pearl of the atom-cosmos, passive on God's finger, I saw also, all around me, though as it were with another vision, the process of cosmical events.

There now came to me a vivid and terrifying realization that between me and the human world which was my true concern there lay aeon upon aeon of cosmical history, and nearly all of it inhuman.

"Oh God," I cried, "let me be again among my own kind. Blot out from my mind the memory of all this irrelevance. Let me play out my little past oblivious of the immensities. Let me take up once more the threads of a life distressed, bewildered, futile, but my own. Let me watch the spectacle of my own world. Futile it may be, tragic it is, but I am shaped for it. And in it there are little creatures like myself whose lives intertwine with mine."

Thus I prayed. But then I remembered the thing that God was, and I knew that it was useless to pray to him; useless, and also, in some manner which I could not comprehend, base.

With a heavy heart I settled myself to the task of watching the bleak and intricate unfolding of the physical cosmos, not as yet feeling its perfection, not as yet realizing that some insight into these remote events was needed to prepare me for insight into the passionate themes which were to follow.

In this book I shall set down only the slightest record of these difficult and wearisome experiences, lest I should inflict on the reader the tedium which I myself suffered, toiling through that desert. But somehow I must entice him at least to fly rapidly with me over the huge wilderness of the early cosmos, and note its features with watchful and interested eyes, so that he may grasp what follows.

By now the unit members of the cosmos, which had first been laid together in one identical volume, were already separated by wide gulfs. Between them was nothing but the tempestuous undulations which they scattered in all directions throughout the cosmos.

These undulations, these ubiquitous light rays, were actually visible to me. Seemingly they were for me illuminated by that other, swifter, more searching and more revealing light, which cast by the lucent person of God himself, pervades and drenches all things.

I could see also the primal members themselves, the radiant centers of all this rippled light. And though they were now once more distinct and scattered, I could see, or rather by a kind of microscopic telepathy I could feel, that each one preserved within itself, like a forgotten memory, the presence and the influence of all the others. Each must now and forever be a true member of the cosmic unity, possessed by the whole, but also pervading the whole with its own unique nature.

Presently I found that I could move hither and thither within the cosmos as I willed, simply by looking in whichever direction I chose to go. Thus, as on the wings of thought, more easily than a bird overtakes a snail, I could outstrip and pass the sluggish lightrays of the cosmos.

Seeing clearly that all things in the cosmos were flying apart from one another, I now set out to seek the boundaries of the ever expanding cosmos. But it turned out that this was a very strange and incomprehensible expansion. For although again and again, and swiftly as thought, I traveled in search of the expanding frontiers, I could not find them. Always my straight course led me continuously through the host of the primal members back to my starting point. The cosmos had no frontiers which could be extended.

Yet as time passed I found upon such journeys that the primal members fell ever further and further apart, or at least that they were ever more minute in comparison with the distances between them. I found also that the light waves of the cosmos took ever longer on their travels before they reached again the points whence they had started.

Thus, after all, the cosmos was in some sense expanding. It was at first a mighty bursting bomb of the jostling members and the tumultuous light; and then a spreading cloud, huge as a galaxy, but congested with the matter and the energies for many million galaxies.

For as it continued to swell it disintegrated into innumerable separate clouds, which sped ever away from one another. At first shoulder to shoulder, they were presently continents separated by oceans; then islands very remote from one another in the boundless and ever more capacious ocean of cosmical space.

Between the clouds, an inconceivably faint mist grew fainter and fainter as the cosmos enlarged itself.

Both clouds and mist were composed of the primal members which God had made. And even in the clouds they were soon as remote from one another, in proportion to their size, as star from star.

And I, who in some other existence am one of the little creatures called men, vermin upon a minute planet of a mediocre star, I who so lately (or in the remote future?) gazed (or should gaze?), tortured but enraptured, into the sad mocking eyes of another of my kind—now drifted, disembodied but percipient, within the unimaginably tenuous sandstorm, snowstorm, pollenstorm of the primaeval cosmos.

The minute simplest members of the cosmos quivered around me like an all-pervading swarm of midges, unpeaceful, fatuous; but vital. With insupportable fatigue I witnessed their endless barren agitation; while the cosmic time settled upon my strained mind softly, irresistibly, without relief, aeon after aeon, like a deepening snowdrift, like that dust which sinks through the oceanic depths year by year, settling to form the rocks of future ages. Never surely was explorer more crushed by monotony and tedium than I, crossing the desert of the earliest cosmical era.

While I was still toiling in this desolation, there came a moment that I realized that I had all along been confronted by something more than the physical aspect of the cosmos, namely its inchoate and profoundly slumbering mentality, in fact by the cumulative impact of the myriad primal mindlets upon my mind. Or should I say the impact of the foetal spirit of the cosmos itself? It matters not which, for at this time the spirit of the cosmos was dissociated into the myriads of the simple spirits of its members.

I was like one who cannot escape from a tiresome companion. But this cosmical companion of mine was legion, and he had entry into my very mind. He quenched my thoughts with the ceaseless murmur of his own vapid, almost featureless experience.

For though with my strange power of microscopic telepathy I could for a while distinguish a few of the individual mindlets, I could discern nothing whatever in their devastatingly similar experiences but the vaguest unrest and the vaguest tactual, or should I say sexual, titillation; nothing but an inconceivably faint and somnolent appetite, which at rare intervals was gratified by an instantaneous orgasm and ejaculation of the divine physical energy.

I could not for long discriminate the individual experiences of the mindlets. Fatique soon blurred my insight. The minute prickling of distinct primal beings against my mind gave place to the confused and indescribably nauseating impression of the whole myriadfold cosmic experience.

In utter boredom and indignation I cursed my fate. Why, why had I been snatched out of the vivid though distressful world of men to be subjected to all this irrelevance? Had I not a life to live, entwined with other lives?

4. The Great Nebulae Appear

I need not have been so despondent, for I was soon
to find myself in a world of passionate beings whose
alien, yet not entirely inhuman nature was to tax my
comprehension and to wring me with conflicting
sympathy and loathing. In a few brief aeons of
cosmical time I was to be the spectator of a drama
the very existence of which my fellow men had never
suspected.

The clouds continued to drift apart from one another, continued to contract and gyrate and define
themselves. Presently they were but small soft
globes or flecks of light, snowflakes whirling in the
huge gulf of space. They seemed to me minute; yet in
each one of them was material for a host of suns, and
worlds innumerable. For these were the Great
Nebulae.

I had at first no inkling that these largest of all
physical objects were alive, that each one of them in
its own unique way was a sensitive and intelligent
being, that every movement of this great host was no
less significant of joy and grief than the gestures and
facial expressions of men and women, that here

31

before me were many which, though possessing nothing at all like a human eye, regarded one another's eloquent forms with joys and longings no less vivid than the personal loves of men and women, and many more which, though blind and deaf to the external world, lived out a strange, passionate yet solipsistic life.

In time I was to learn, through long and difficult experience, not only to understand these beings up to a point, but also to respect them. But how can I give by means of a few printed pages the insight which I myself took aeons to acquire? There is nothing for it but to beg the reader once more to have patience while I try to describe as briefly as possible the physical and mental nature of the great nebulae. For without understanding the great difference between nebular and human nature he cannot possibly appreciate the strange and moving story which will follow.

In the earliest age of nebular history, when the expansion of the cosmos was not yet far advanced, the nebulae were very much closer to one another than in the age of man. They were also far more numerous; for many, as I shall tell, have been destroyed, and their flesh converted into energy to carry out the all too human activities of their fellows. They were also, at this time, much less evenly distributed than in our day. Most lay even now remote from all neighbors, lone sails on the ocean. These were the "lone nebulae" which spent their formative youth each in its own solipsistic universe. Others voyaged in convoy of a dozen or a score, or eddied together in shoals of hundreds or even a thousand. Here and there a leviathan made progress amid encircling satellites. These minute satellite nebulae constituted a race apart. Of one individual I shall say much at a later stage. Like their larger companions they were destined in the fullness of time to crumble into stars; but they would form not huge galaxies but the crowded swarms which we call the globular clusters.

Already the normal nebulae were very diverse. Some were greater, some smaller; some mere smudges of mist, some compact and formal. Each feathery ball, I noticed, was slowly shrinking. And as it shrank, it whirled more rapidly. And as it whirled, it was flattened. And as the flattening continued, there appeared in the center a bright and swollen core. The outer parts of the nebula were flung by their own movement far out into space; but seemingly the tugging core still kept a hold on them, so that they developed into an attenuated disc around the heart of the nebula, and were torn into streamers and spreading convolutions. So might a dancer, pirouetting, halo her bright head with far-flung, tangled whirls.

Such at least was the form of these nebulae that were too far apart to distort one another. But those that were members of compact groups expressed by their very deformity their dependence upon one another. As woodland trees mold one another, so these great clouds, though at a distance of several light-years, molded one another with their tidal sway.

It was an unearthly but a rich and subtle spectacle that now confronted me on every side. With slow rhythmic movements, the airy creatures floated around me delicately featured with many colors imperceptible to the normal human eye. Their cores were mostly tinged with violet or blue, their tresses nacrous gray, iridescent with green and gold and crimson and many unimaginable hues. In every direction and at every depth they appeared, the most distant as a very faint host of misty points. Between them spread the deep, the absolute blackness of the void.

The nearer nebulae reminded me ever more forcibly of living things. They displayed even that appearance of intelligence and purpose which is manifested by animalcules on a microscope slide. They were in continual oozy movement. I could imagine that they were seeking food, or some needed but unconceived fulfillment. Sometimes they would seem to pursue and avoid one another. Occasionally a giant would absorb and assimilate a dwarf. Or two peers, after long lonely voyaging, would come within close range of one another and protrude, each toward the other, a searching excrescence, as though yearning for intercourse. Sometimes the contact would fail to be achieved, or would be a mere moth's kiss, and the two would be borne apart with altered forms and courses. Sometimes the "lovers" would meet and mingle, to become a single great and brilliant organism, which, a pike among the small-fry, would proceed to devour all that crossed its path.

Could these lifelike creatures, I asked myself, be mere vortices of radiant gas? But I reminded myself that the briefest of the movements which I now witnessed must in fact occupy millions of terrestrial years, and that this impression of vital activity was an illusion. Age upon age must pass, I knew, before these clouds would condense into stars, and further ages before the rare meetings of stars should produce habitable worlds.

Why, I wondered, should God so long toy with lifeless matter before undertaking the main purpose of his work? And why should I, forlorn little terrestrial intelligence, be forced to watch this aimless, this puerile sport?

But at last I began to realize that, all unnoticed, new and strange experience had for some time been welling up within me, and was now clamoring for recognition.

Out of the confused and fatuous mumur of the primal mindlets of the cosmos there had emerged something new and uncouth and formidable. To use an image, the shrill and monotonous pipings of innumerable midges had been drowned by the boisterous incantation of a hurricane; or was it some more significant music, unintelligible to me?

Columbus, when he stumbled on a new world, a world of novel vegetation, beasts and men, cannot have been half so bewildered as I, who now found myself inwardly confronted by this new world of alien and primaeval spirits.

My poor human mind was at first overstrained and tortured by the flood of uncouth perceptions and novel hungers and fears which now flooded in upon me. But little by little, with many timorous tastings and agonized revulsions, I was able to accommodate myself so far as to receive without undue stress at least a muted and schematic echo of the mentality that had at first so jarred me. To do this, I had first to discriminate within the general babel some one theme of experience, the life story of some particular nebula. Attending to this, I found that the rest faded into the background, leaving me free to study, if I dared, and if I could endure it, the ardent and voluminous experience of being fantastically alien to man.

By what laborious and often painful experiment I learned at length to range at will among the minds of the nebulae, even as, with physical vision I could look now at this airy creature, now at that, I need not tell. Nor need I recount the long drawn out research by which I passed from sheer incomprehension to some degree of understanding of the nebular mentality. Instead I will present at once the fruits of my toil. I will at once try to give some idea first of the nature and then of the impassioned history of these most immense of all living creatures. It is a history which reaches its climax before the first stars were born, and it is not completed even in our own age of terrestrial intelligence.

5. A Biological Study

The newborn nebulae existed for aeons as mere lucent clouds of gas, featureless and mindless. But when within each flattening globe a bright dense core had appeared, this came to rule the whole mass with its preponderant sway, and with the ceaseless and violent outrush of its radiation.

And presently, when the primal beings within the core had become very crowded, and very subject to mutual influence and to the overmastering tempest of light on which they were tossed, there was formed, deep within the incandescent heart of the core itself, a unifying center of life, a region no larger than the bulk of a thousand stars, but dense almost as a liquid, and turbulent with such fury of radiation as had not occurred since the atom-cosmos first responded to God's word.

Within this boiling cauldron of the divine physical energy, within this tense and enduring system of intricate currents, antagonized yet cooperative, within this vast germ cell set in the vaster yoke of the nebular core, the new vital order was mysteriously welded, and the myriad dissociated primal beings were at last harnessed and domesticated for the support and service of a theme of spirit more admirable than their own, namely for the embryonic mind of the nebula.

Little by little, this vital center organized the whole core as a balanced yet ever-changing system of hurricanes, trade winds, tornadoes, subservient in all their operations to the vital needs of the whole.

And as the airy streamers and filaments of the nebular disc began to appear, these also were inwardly organized to the requirements of the new being. They became in fact true living tissues, fulfilling all manner of delicate vital functions, though they were but ordered winds, more tenuous than any man-made "vacuum." Strange that such loose-knit material could form the body of such a vivid spirit!

It is not surprising that I could not discover the mechanism of this steady internal evolution. But one point seemed to me certain. Natural selection played an important part within each nebula, favoring some experiments in vital organization and destroying others, much as on earth it favors some races of organisms and destroys others.

The living nebula has no need to gather energy from the world outside its own substance. Its font of power lies in the very matter which is its flesh. Its hunting ground and its prey are within its own intestines. It feeds upon its own secretion. For the primal beings within it provide by their myriadfold ejaculations a lavish source of power.

Thus the living nebula is exempt from that necessity which is of the first but not of the highest importance to every terrestrial creature, namely the need to reach out into the environment for light and food. Yet in spite of this heaven-sent exemption, there was to come a time when it would be flung away, and the whole cosmical community of nebulae would be shattered by conflict over mechanical power.

In spite of deep differences, the nebulae and the living things of earth are at bottom akin, for in each the prime vital tendency and the most urgent desire are directed toward self-maintenance and development; and in both kinds of life there is needed for this end a constant flow of energy. Further, just as for terrestrial creatures the procuring of physical energy is the main practical enterprise, so in the living nebula the first of all tasks is to secure to its own vital processes a lavish supply of its own internal radiation. But the nebula's task is in one respect the easier and in another the more difficult. It never suffers from dearth but the torrential violence of its own energy spate is apt to rend and shatter its flimsy tissues.

Since they have no need to seek food abroad or to avoid being preyed upon, none of the young nebulae save those significant few which grow up in enduring groups, develop organs of external sense. For the lone nebula, experience is entirely of events within its own body. But of those internal events it develops a very poignant and subtle awareness. It has an urgent need to be sensitive to the fluctuations of its internal energies, so that it may control and organize their expression and prevent them from damaging its tissues. So varied and inconstant are the patterns of events within the great fluid body, that physiological controls are seldom automatic, as they are with us, but almost always under conscious and intelligent guidance.

The core and the tresses of the living nebula are composed of many kinds of tissues, each a pattern of little enduring whirlwinds of many gasses and dusts in physical relation with one another. Scattered through these tissues are many organs of sensation and of control, and many insulated tracks for the transmission of messages between the core and the tresses. By means of this complex organization the nebula becomes very precisely aware of the intricate pattern of events which constitute its bodily life, and it influences them very minutely according to its wishes. It is sensitive to all the frequencies of radiation, to pressure, to warmth and cold and to many chemical changes. It can retard and quicken the flow of its radiation in different parts of its body. It can also, by stimulating certain regions to expand or contract, alter the shape of its convolutions.

Since a nebula is so large that the cosmical light takes many thousands of years to travel across it, its nerve currents, though moving at the speed of light, are in a sense very sluggish. The whole tempo of nebular life is therefore, from the human point of view, fantastically slow. Passages of thought which a human brain would perform in a few seconds would take the huge nebular brain many years. Yet in terms of its own life its mental operations are rapid. "Quick as thought" is an analogy as true for the nebula as for man. For slow as its thinking seems to us, its responses to events occurring in its remote extremities are far slower. In dealing with such events it has to take into account time lost on the inward and outward passage of the nerve current, just as we, when we carry on a correspondence, have to take into account time lost in the post.

Owing to the extreme slowness of their experience, the nebulae tend to be much impressed by the swiftness and elusive changefulness of events. And when at last, after aeons of maturity, they begin to notice in themselves that decay which we associate with senescence, they are dismayed at the brevity of their life.

In its earliest phase the foetal mind of the nebula hovers long between the deepest slumber and drowsy waking. It basks in its own inherent sunshine. It luxuriates in the confused streaming and stroking and thrusting of its living winds, as they move among one another on their ordered courses. But as the ages pass, it comes to feel more accurately its patterned currents and the spreading torrents of its radiation; and little by little it takes charge of its own economy. It has by now perceptions not only of light and darkness, pressures, balance, and a thousand tactual textures, but also of vigor, faintness, fatigue, restlessness, the glow of health, and innumerable local strains and pains. These manifold characters it experiences with all the precision which we know only in perceiving the external world. It inwardly feels and sees its body in more detail than we achieve in touching and seeing external objects. But of its environment it knows less than we know of our digestive operations.

As a human infant, lying in its cot, discovers its toes and exults in dictating their movements, so the infant nebula discovers not toes and fingers, ears and genitals, but the living and mobile tresses that are its limbs. But whereas the human infant discovers its body's external aspect and at the same time sets about exploring the vast external world, the lone nebulae is externally blind and numb. Yet internally it encounters such diversified and passionate experience, that in many cases, though this may seem almost incredible, the lone nebulae have developed a considerable intricacy of thought and a vast and subtle gamut of emotions. I shall later try to give some idea of this strange life.

The mental life of the lone nebulae had of course to be carried on entirely without the use of language. That it could proceed at all, thus hobbled, may seem impossible. But I found that the more advanced of the lone nebulae had, as a matter of fact, been driven to develop a kind of "internal language" of symbolic images and incipient gestures. In many cases this proved a very efficient vehicle for the process of their thought and feeling.

Only the relatively few nebulae which were "born" in groups developed normally any perception of events occurring beyond their own bodies. For these it was very important to react to the whole group in which they lived, for they had far-reaching influences on one another, determining their mutual orbits, shaping each other, with their tidal attraction, sometimes tearing limbs from one another, sometimes caressing one another, sometimes fighting to the death, sometimes ecstatically merging.

Even in infancy the social nebulae began to be mutually sensitive. Their external perceptions were derived from experience of the distortion of their vital form by the gravitational sway of their neighbors, and from light which impinged upon their outer tissues.

I need not tell in detail how, from the direction, strength and texture of these external influences, the young social nebulae came to apprehend one another as physical objects. Their visual perceptions were of course very different from those which we obtain by lens and retina. Their grasp of the solid form of seen objects was based on their power of discriminating slight differences in the direction of the light rays which entered their tissues at different points. Thus their seeing consisted of the apprehension of innumerable ever-changing parallaxes, the relations of which were automatically analyzed in the brain tracts of the core, and perceived as external objects having precise shapes and colors and sizes, and moving at definite distances from the point of vision.

When I had succeeded in mastering this odd way of seeing, I found it no less subtle and no less aesthetically significant than the familiar human mode.

The nebula's sense of external attraction was at bottom not unlike a blend of our touch, our balance, and our kinaesthesis. But it was developed with the same subtlety as nebular vision. It afforded very precise perceptions of masses at a distance, discriminating them with surprising accuracy in respect of shape and detailed texture of density. Thus it amounted to a kind of "tactual seeing" entirely unknown to man.

In addition to these two ways of perceiving one another, the social nebulae could sense differences of electric charge in their neighbors. And as electric changes were symptomatic of emotional changes, this electric sensitivity had for the percipient a strong emotive significance.

Along with powers of external perception came powers of voluntary locomotion. In infancy the nebula's orbit was determined solely by the simpler principles which we call physical. But as the young creatures developed needs to avoid and approach one another, they acquired also, litle by little, the power to control their movements. This was done by directing the discharge of their radiation in such a manner that the recoil might propel them whither they willed. At first this voluntary control produced but a slight perturbation of the normal orbit, but in time it came to be used with greater effect. It was not until the discovery of mechanical power, the subatomic energy derived from the disintegration of the flesh of their slaughtered fellows, that the social nebulae were able to make long voyages from group to group.

The social nebulae could communicate with one another. In infancy they learned to associate certain appearances of their neighbors with impending approach or flight, hostility or friendliness, vigor or fatigue, and so on. In time they came to make deliberate use of these spontaneous "gestures" to communicate their intentions to one another. And from these clumsy babblings of childhood each group of nebulae developed in maturity a more or less efficient language, which grew up in close association with the internal "language" of symbolic images and movements. The external language in its finished state consisted entirely of delicate rhythmic changes of radiation produced and received by specialized organs.

6. Outline of a Strange Mentality

To understand the mentality of the nebulae, one must bear in mind three facts which make them differ through and through from human beings. They do not succeed one another in generations; they are not constrained by economic necessity; the great majority of them have reached maturity in ignorance of other minds.

On Earth, the individuals of a race procreate and die, handing on the torch of evolution and of tradition to their successors. But with the nebulae there is no distinction between the growth of individuals and the evolution of the race. The life and memory of each nebula reaches back to the racial dawn. The race consists of the original host of individuals that condensed more or less contemporaneously after the explosion of the atom-cosmos. When the last of these dies, the race dies with it.

Nebular evolution has consequently been far less profuse in "experimental" types than terrestrial evolution. It has not proliferated in myriad diverse species. Its advance has been more steady and less varied. It was partly through this lack of variety,

47

partly through the extreme simplicity of the environment (compared with the immense complexity of our terrestrial environment) that even the social nebulae developed a certain naive directness of thought and feeling known only in human children. Owing to this lack of sophistication nebular history displays more starkly and dramatically than human history the great formative influences at work within it.

Another important consequence of the absence of generations is this. The nebulae are in a sense "nearer to God" than any man can ever be. The human child, in spite of our great poet, trails but dim and tattered clouds of glory. He embarks upon life, not fresh from God's making fingers, but warped by the misfortunes and blunders of countless ancestors; and, no sooner is he born, than he entangles himself further by learning from the example of his elders. But the nebulae wake with the divine lust keen and unconfused within them, and they pursue it untrammeled either by errant instinct or by perverse tradition. Never need they suffer from mistakes not their own, or be led astray by the half-truths of teachers whose very obscurity lends them a baneful prestige. Thus the nebulae, at least in their youthful phase, have been able on the whole to follow the light within them with a steadier will than man, though with less diversity of expression. Stage by stage during their youth, and without any widespread misadventure, they have discovered the true direction of their nature, and have very constantly pursued it. Not till the main host of them was already in the prime was fate to waylay them with an opportunity of destroying themselves by offering them the priceless but dangerous gift of mechanical power.

The absence of generations had another far-reaching effect. In all human cultures the idea of parenthood, birth and death, and all the attributes of youth and age, are familiar and significant. But the nebulae in their early maturity, before they began to conceive their cosmical society, were almost entirely without these experiences. Parenthood and birth were the rarest accidents; death itself was on the whole an unusual calamity, always artificially produced, and common only in periods of warfare. Youth they knew vaguely from recollection of their past phases and the study of their less mature contemporaries. Senescence was as yet not even a rare disease. It was entirely unknown. Not till the last phase of the nebular drama did they discover the inexorable decay and annihilation which plays so great a part in all human experience.

No less important than the absence of generations was lack of constraint by economic necessity. Interest in economic activities, which has played a part in terrestrial life at once so stimulating to the practical intelligence and so hostile to the finer kinds of percipience and thought, finds no place in nebular culture. When at last (as I shall tell) sheer intellectual curiosity stumbled upon the means of utilizing subatomic energy, and militarism found a use for it, economic activity did indeed play a great part in the nebular world; but even then, and even though it brought disaster, it was never (as so often with us) taken to be an end. It was always emphatically subordinated to the true and universally accepted goal of nebular life, a goal which unfortunately the human mind can only very dimly conceive.

Until I became familiar with nebular life I had supposed that without the spur of economic need no progress could be made, and the higher reaches of mentality would never be achieved. This error seems to me now ludicrous.

In the young nebulae another stimulus took the place of the economic; and in those that were mature the habit of ardent endeavor persisted, though its original cause had ceased. Not the need to annex energy, but the need to canalize it so that it should do no damage to the vital organization, was the stimulus to practical activity. All nebulae at every age, but especially in youth and early maturity, are beset by the fear that at any moment they may fail to maintain the structure of their airy tissues and organs. For not only the violence of radiation, but also any sudden voluntary movement, if too vigorous or jerky, may rend them; as with a mere breath one may disintegrate a smoke wreath. Thus all nebulae live in constant dread of physical disorders and mental derangements of the most terrifying kind. And all in their youth have to behave with courage and intelligence in order to cope with these dangers. As terrestrial animals delight in hunting and feasting and fighting, so the young nebulae delight to conquer and tame the fury of radiation within their dense cores. But again and again I have seen, and actually felt, their delicate organs wounded in untoward adventures. In some cases life itself has been destroyed, perhaps to appear again after aeons of quiescence, perhaps to remain forever extinguished.

More often the damage would be painfully repaired by conscious remolding of the wounded parts, and the only scar would be a memory of horror. Sometimes, though life maintained itself, intelligence was abolished; and the unhappy creature must henceforth drift through space forever torturing itself with insane fantasies.

This precariousness of life breeds in the young nebulae something of that directness and heroism which we look for in primitive human societies. But whereas with us the active and "realist" temperament is all too prone to be snared into the pursuit of gross material power, in the nebulae it can as a rule find no such outlet and must instead expend itself in perfecting the vital organization and the instruments of mental life.

The last of the three most important facts for the understanding of nebular mentality is the complete isolation of very many nebulae throughout their youth. Social life was impossible to them. And since self-consciousness depends very largely on the conscious distinction between self and others, this also was unable to develop normally in the isolated nebulae. Only when disease produced in them violent mental conflicts and a state of "multiple personality" did they ever conceive of a plurality of minds. And then, of course, it was regarded by them not as affording the possibility of love and all the loveliest blossoms of the spirit, but as a hideous distemper; which indeed it was.

Yet an extremely complex inner life has combined with freedom from economic servitude to foster in them a kind of self-consciousness peculiar to themselves. They had no opportunity of distinguishing between "I" and "you"; but they had constant need of distinguishing between "I" and the many opposed and often rebellious processes and cravings at work within them. Though normally they could never conceive the possibility of an "ego" or a "stream of consciousness" other than their own, they thoroughly grasped the difference between the lowly and the lofty within themselves.

Moreover, owing to lack of distraction, they were able to apprehend earlier, and to develop more earnestly, certain aspects of "inner" experience or "experience *of* experience" which terrestrial spirits can only rarely and with austere self-discipline discover at all. I myself, very surely, could never have appreciated this side of nebular life had I not suffered an agelong process of self-discipline under the influence of my cosmical adventure. And now that the adventure is over, and I try to record it, I find that I have lost the insight which was then forced upon me.

Lack of inherited complexity and of cultural sophistication, lack of economic adventures, and lack of social experience combined to give to the lone nebulae an innocence and single-mindedness which at first I mistook for sheer mental poverty. I had long savored the minds of many mature nebulae before I began to understand what it was that they were seeking to do with their lives. And even when I had gained some insight into their passionately sought, but to my mind "one-dimensional" ideals, aeons had yet to pass before activities which I had hitherto regarded with condescension, sometimes even with disgust, began to display a characteristic beauty and a mysterious, nay, a mystical, significance.

As the young nebula advances to maturity, its constitution becomes more hardy and its practical activity more regular and automatic. It now seeks fresh modes of expression. To my surprise I discovered that time and interest were henceforth increasingly given to a strange kind of internal play. For no practical end, but for sheer delight, the great kittenish creature would juggle its living winds into freakish patterns, or thread them together as meshes of interwoven currents. Or it would toss and ripple its flying tresses for sheer joy of "muscular" skill.

This phase of carefree sportive behavior, I observed, might be brief or lengthy or even perennial. But in the career of every normal nebula there occurred sooner or later a stage when the life of play began to pall, and the mind was invaded by strange images and formless longings.

In many respects this phase is like human adolescence. The zest of play would steadily fade, and the vigorous young creature would be vaguely longing for new worlds to conquer.

For a while, sometimes indeed for aeons, the nebula would now vacillate between sheer indolence and bouts of fantastic play, more difficult and dangerous than the normal kind. In this stage many a vital but foolhardy young nebula has lost its life or crashed into insanity. Yet even the most intricate and daring sport has failed to satisfy. Only the most obtuse, the most coarse-grained nebular minds have persuaded themselves that sheer physical prowess and physical courage were able to fulfill the obscure demands of their nature. And even in these I found no real contentment, but a never consciously recognized despair.

The main character of nebular adolescence was a surprised zest which could never find full expression. It was as though in all experience there was not a new and teasing flavor, a hint, never fulfilled, of some exquisite way of life awaiting discovery. I was reminded of certain moments of my own youth when I was suddenly and unaccountably seized with a conviction that the secret of existence was about to be made plain to me. But in the young nebula this sense of impending revelation was not fleeting and occasional but an enduring state that dominated the whole behavior.

As the ages passed, and the main host of the nebulae advanced each toward its lonely maturity, one or two seemed to discover the solution of their problem. For after a long spell of almost complete quiescence they plunged into resolute and costly action, at first confused, and then sustained and orderly. Savoring their experience, I found that they were now in a state of fervent endeavor and exaltation. In time almost the whole company was thus occupied, each isolated individual passionately striving after an ideal of self-expression in complete ignorance of the rest. Only in the comparatively rare social nebulae did adolescence take a different turn.

When I examined more closely the kind of behavior which the isolated nebulae were now pursuing so

ardently, I could not at first make anything of it. When I tried to discover in their minds intelligible sources of their exaltation, I was defeated.

Patiently, but with increasing hostility and contempt, I now watched the incomprehensible antics of these hugest creatures. I had been able to appreciate their play, simply as unpretentious play; but this passionate devotion to a seemingly barren athletic skill nauseated me even more than the vapid mentality of the primal units. Surely these nebular minds, which I knew to have percipience and intelligence to a high degree, were capable of some richer life!

That the activity called for courage, I recognized, for many a nebula, confronted by some desperate crisis in its athletic adventure, gallantly took the course demanded by its insane ideal, and was destroyed. That skill of a high order was demanded was no less obvious, for as I watched I discovered the main principles which governed this strange occupation and was over and over again amazed at the ingenuity with which, in seemingly hopeless circumstances, they were fulfilled. But why, why was all this courage and skill exercised in so puerile a manner?

In time, something of the truth began to dawn on me. I began to realize that for the nebulae this passionate athleticism was pure art of the highest order. It was not, after all, a subtle and inverted kind of self-indulgence, a sort of masturbatory ecstasy, a lethal sop to the ever hungry and lonely spirit. No, for these strange beings this was indeed the way of life, the straight and narrow way. And age by age, as

I watched, I myself came to enter sympathetically into it.

All the detailed action and the governing principles of this fantastic terpsichorean display derived a profound symbolism from associations in the age-long nebular past experience. The whole matter and the whole form of this art was deeply significant. By playing upon the secret strings of the past, it wakened the nebular mind to a new order of percipience for the future. What I had regarded as barren athleticism, no more significant than the slavery of golf or football, turned out to be in fact something which combined the nature of abstract art with the nature of ritualistic dancing.

I was amazed and not a little humiliated to find that I, who had so recently pitied the isolation and self-absorbtion of these imprisoned spirits, had now to learn from them. With mingled awe and discontent I now wandered from one hermit mind to another, allowing each in turn to dominate me with the strange impersonal yet passionate music of its life. Their creations differed in form and mood with all the diversity of human art. Some were naive, some subtle; some more passionate, some more formal, and so on. But in all those that had successfully passed beyond the initiate stages I found the same identical ecstasy.

7. The Social Nebulae

It was with mingled awe and amusement that I ranged among the many groups of the social nebulae, awe at the vast and stormy universe into which I had fallen, amusement at the blend of the fantastic and the human in their behavior.

At this early stage of cosmical expansion, groups of nebulae having constant intercourse were common. Moreover, there was occasional intercourse between groups. One small family or great tribe would drift within "speaking distance" of another, and signals would pass between them, at first unintelligible. More rarely, two groups would actually collide. Each would then desperately seek to preserve its own group life and bend the other to its will. Sometimes, a number of groups, drifting more or less in proximity along the same stream (so to speak) of cosmical movement, would grow up as a community of separate clans, possessing in spite of local differences a common basis of culture, though no common allegiance. In these groups of groups intertribal warfare was perennial.

But most groups of nebulae throughout the cosmos grew up to maturity in complete isolation from one

another. Not till certain exceptionally favored
groups began to feel curiosity about the more remote
objects around them was any attempt made to communicate by light signals between the groups. Not
till the utilization of subatomic power was there any
possibility of voyaging from group to group.

All nebulae, social and solitary alike, are so fashioned as to find their deepest satisfaction in dance-
like physical activity internal and external. At the
lowliest this terpsichorean behavior is sheer animal
play, but at its loftiest it is best described as pure art
of a peculiarly subtle and powerful kind. By its
veiled creative symbolism this art, as I have said,
can raise the nebular spirit to the highest reaches of
religious ecstasy. In the social nebulae the dance life
is of course socialized and pregnant with all manner
of social symbolism. In the solitary nebulae its aim is
simply the perfection of self-expression.

Among the social nebulae, as among human beings, there arose inevitably all kinds of conflicts
between the individual perfection and the social
perfection. But in the nebular world these conflicts
often took forms unknown on Earth.

With the nebulae the conflict was always at bottom an aesthetic conflict between the individual
dance rhythm and the social dance rhythm. Each
social individual experienced the urge to aesthetic
self-perfection; but also he recognized, grudgingly or
with delight, the rights of others to their own aesthetic policies, and the aesthetic excellence of the
group itself.

Sometimes an unfortunate solitary nebula would
happen to drift within range of a group and would be

seized upon by the members of the group, either in the hope of gaining his support for one social party against another, or, if the group were a harmonious one, simply for the embellishment of the group by the presence of an interesting and beautiful foreigner. For the lone nebulae, being exempt from external influences, attained a perfection of physical form which was ever a source of wonder to the social nebulae. The captured solitary would of course prove quite incapable even of realizing that the shocking distortions and agonies which now beset him were caused by the efforts of other minds to communicate with him. It would very soon appear to the social nebulae that, for all his physical perfection and symmetry, the foreigner was but an abject savage, unable to appreciate the beauties of group life, and incapable even of intelligent intercourse; in fact, that he was a mere brute, physically superb, but blind, deaf, and incredibly stupid. For to the excited and babbling observers he offered no hint of the strange solipsistic intelligence and will at work within him.

Sometimes the stranger would be forcibly retained within the group as a curiosity, like a beast in a zoo. But more often he would be roughly expelled as a mere irrelevance in the group pattern. Probably he would be so mauled in body and shattered in mind by the hurricane of incomprehensible experiences, that the upshot for him would be either insanity or death.

The social life of the nebulae impressed me with extraordinary vividness because it was so clearly embodied in perceptual and aesthetic forms. I could actually *see* the conflict between the individual and the group. I could see the individual struggling to maintain the symmetry and the spontaneous rhythms of his own body against the compulsive and distorting influences of the group. Also, it must be remembered, I could *feel* in his mind the two conflicting apprehensions of beauty. I could savor both his passion for the lyrical freedom of his own dance life, and his ecstatic self-subjection to the dance life of the group as a whole.

I could enter into his personal loves and hates, too, all the more vividly because, in time, I became sensitive to the perceptual harmonies and discords between the private dance rhythms of diverse individuals. When I had been so immersed in nebular life that I could appreciate the exquisite expressiveness of nebular forms and actions, it became visually patent to me that such and such a nebular mind must inevitably be enthralled by the sight of such and such a beauty of tresses and core; or that such and such a style or mode or mannerism in the dance life of one individual must to the vision of a certain other individual be significant of a base spirit.

The nebulae, I found, were capable of every kind of personal relationship known to us. Even sexual partnership had its counterpart among these asexual beings. For though there were not two definite sexual types, many dance unions included physical caresses, and even a transmission of substance from individual to individual, for mutual invigoration, though not for procreation.

As with human beings, so with nebulae, love was broadly of two kinds. There was a simple love hunger directed upon any individual that promised enrichment to the pattern of one's own life. This kind of love led often to partnerships between two or three nebulae, each of which sought merely personal enrichment from the union, each of which willed merely to impose on the partnership his own aesthetic ideal. Needless to say, the result of such unions was invariably disaster. There was also love that included genuine admiration of the other's physical beauty and prowess, or of his mental or moral perfection. Sometimes, indeed, this passion was so intense that the lover dared not approach at all near to the beloved for fear of marring his beauty by his own extraneous gravitational sway. But in the happiest cases, where admiration and desire were mutual, each would conceive a craving to complete his own form by responding to the other's influence.

The most impressive of all nebular societies were those few small communities in which all the members were thus inwardly united by bonds of mutual understanding and affection, and all were also constantly, and sometimes passionately, raised above the individual plane by a common social purpose, namely the will to work out together an ever more harmonious and more significant dance life for the whole group.

Very few groups attained this perfection. Most were either too closely or too loosely knit. In the former the individual spirit was stifled by the proximity of his neighbors. He was a mere herd member, with no inner being. And because society was composed of barren individuals, social life was barren also. The dance pattern of the group was, so to speak, geometrical and fatuous. In the too loosely knit groups, on the other hand, there was no willed community at all, but only a grudging contract by which all engaged to refrain from interference with their neighbors, so as to secure the maximum freedom of individual behavior.

In very many cases the group was perenially torn between two or more parties with opposing aims. One, for instance, might be seeking a more free and open formation of the group life, the other a dance form more close-knit and disciplined, in which every individual's shape and activity should be through and through determined by the pattern of the whole. Or one party might strive for an aristocratic society of dance leaders with satellites, the other for a more democratic arrangement. One might wish to see the group life controlled by predominantly athletic principles, another might demand a more genuine aesthetic mode, another might wish to subordinate the pure aesthetic to the religious in the significance of the dance. In a few groups there were intellectualists who wished to subordinate all activity to theoretical enquiry into the mysteries of physical and mental phenomena.

Sometimes in a group torn by conflicts or oppressed by some powerful oligarchy an individual with a strong urge toward self-perfection would seek to escape from the group into outer space, purposing to live the life of a hermit. Or a couple or triplet of ardent lovers would try to break away from the prying and tyrannously moral supervision of their fellows. Or an oppressed aesthetic or religious sect would seek to found an independent society. But seldom did the fugitives attain their end. Either by physical violence or by subtle moral pressure they would be compelled to remain and to subordinate the pattern of their lives even more rigorously than before to the dance rhythms of the groups.

In some groups I found two parties identical in disposition and policy in all respects save that each considered that itself should rule and the other be a subject race. In some others, one party, through long subjection, had lost the power of independent choice and had become inherently servile. In extreme cases the subject race was so debased that they were mere cattle under the control of the master race. And often the masters themselves were by now so modified in actual physical constitution that, had their slaves deserted them, they would have been undone; for little by little they had come to effect a style of athleticism and even a physiological habit which would have broken down completely if menial service had ceased to be available. Their dance measures were so difficult, their bodily constitution and mental operations so subtle and precarious, that they needed constant assistance from the simpler, tougher, and automatically loyal "cattle" attendant on them.

One other kind of group should be mentioned, namely that in which a great nebula imposed its dance measures on a number of minute satellites. These little creatures, which were as a rule bald cores shorn of all tresses, were generally unable to advance beyond that grade of consciousnes which we attribute to our simian relatives. They were indeed mere domestic animals, unintelligent dance minions to the dominant partner; and mostly they were

treated with no more consideration than our backward races expend on their cattle and poultry. But a
few of these satellite nebulae, wrought and tempered
by exceptional circumstances, developed a keen and
fearless intellect such as the normal nebulae seldom
attained. And one member of this dwarf race made
history upon the grandest scale.

8. The Martial Groups

In most nebular societies, at one time or other in their career, conflict between opposed parties would flare up into actual warfare. One side would seek to overcome the other either by bombarding their most vulnerable organs with concentrated radiation, or by actually grappling with them and striving to tear them into fragments.

It is difficult to give any idea of the horror with which I observed these battles. Superficially the spectacle was nothing but a confused tempest of whirling gas clouds in the depths of space; but to me, who had by now learned the emotional significance of all these changing shapes, to me who moreover could experience at first hand the agony of these torn tresses and shattered cores, the spectacle was no less nerve-racking than the sight of human bodies dismembered by shellfire.

Though not wholly unknown among the normal groups, war was a comparatively rare disaster. But there was one very remarkable kind of group in which fighting was perennial, and indeed essential to the group life. A permanent peace would have brought about a far-reaching degeneration of the individual character and the end of all social feeling, which in these groups could never assume any form but that of the comradeship of brothers-in-arms, opposed by a common foe.

This state of affairs was the result of causes in the remote past. Sometimes the group was in origin a composite of two groups which had collided long ago in the time when the nebulae were still young and mentally unformed. Whatever the cause, the individuals in these martial groups had specialized little by little both physically and mentally for combat. If combat was long denied them, they tended to become morbidly depressed; and ultimately each would succumb to serious mental disorder, snatching a crazy gratification for its pugnacity from the internal conflict of its own dissociated personalities.

In these curiously bellicose communities there sometimes arose a truly astounding culture unlike anything known on earth, though containing suggestions of mediaeval chivalry and modern sport. The opposing forces would be precisely matched, each individual of one troop having a special opponent in the other. Though each warrior might on occasion fight any member of the enemy force, one particular enemy was his peculiar property, his *"dear* enemy." In combat with this individual he not only rose to the extreme of fury or cold hate, but also he attained a unique exaltation which might almost as well be called love as hate, since it included, along with the lust to destroy, a chivalrous and passionate admiration of the foe. This strange movement of the spirit was accompanied at its height by a violent physical orgasm which ejaculated a murderous flood of radiation into the body of the enemy and reduced the subject himself to exhaustion.

In these martial groups there was often a very complicated etiquette of war, meticulously respected by both sides. Life in such a group consisted of personal combats, general warfare, and spells of highly militarized peace. Combats had always a ritual element in them, and were of many degrees of seriousness, from the ceremonial joust to the death struggle. Even the most lethal fighting was terpsichorean in intention, reminiscent at once of the ballroom and the ballet, the football match and the boxing ring, the gladiatorial show, the bullfight, and the sadistic rituals of primitive human societies.

Though the strife was strictly regulated and sincerely aesthetic, it was definitely lethal in intention. In the earlier stages of nebular evolution the opposing warriors could do little serious hurt to one another, but as they advanced in knowledge of physical nature they discovered how to utilize in combat some of the lavish excess of radiation which was constantly issuing from their cores and wasting itself in the void. By damming the flow, and then releasing it in concentrated and focused beams they were able to do one another grievous hurt. The side which was first in the field with the new weapon was duly execrated by the enemy, who then hastened to adopt the same device. Very soon the etiquette of the group was modified to accommodate it, and war went smoothly on, till some fresh improvement was discovered. This, in turn, was execrated and adopted.

Now it sometimes happened that one side used its new weapon so effectively that it soon found itself in a position to destroy the enemy. But as soon as this possibility was realized by an intelligent victor, he would declare peace and set about salving the host which he had come so near exterminating. Sometimes, if the enemy had suffered many fatal casualties, certain members of the victorious host would be drafted into the defeated army. At all costs the vanquished must be strengthened, so that they might become once more an adequate foe.

I was struck by two great differences between militarized man and the militarized nebulae. In man the militarization of the individual mind is never as thorough as in the nebulae. His devotion to warfare is never so singleminded. His unmilitary nature is even liable to betray him into phases of pacifism. But in the finest examples of nebular militarism, Mars was worshipped with complete devotion. Only in those groups in which, through the exigencies of fortune, there remained traces of the impulses toward a pacific dance form, or toward mutual service, or toward intellectual pursuits, was the dance of war ever liable to be marred.

The second respect in which nebular militarism differed from our own was this. The nebulae, since they could not propagate their kind, could not rely on an inexhaustible supply of the raw material of slaughter. The average group had only a few hundred members. It was impossible, therefore, not to regret the killing of an enemy, since, once killed, he could never be killed again. It was even regrettable that an enemy should ever be permanently maimed, since as a cripple he could never again be a worthy foe.

But such was the spirit of the militarized nebulae that these regrets were seldom allowed to interfere with the prosecution of the noble dance of war. Only in a few debased groups was war emasculated by the convention that lethal weapons should not be used. In most, the process of mutual slaughter proceeded honorably and steadily; though slowly, for in nebular warfare improvements in defense managed to keep pace with improvements in attack. In many of the martial groups the members were well aware that extinction faced them; but they were convinced that one hour of glorious life was worth an age without a name. Not once but many times have I watched the final scene of such a heroic drama. The last two surviving heroes, locked in graceful but murderous embrace, and surrounded by the corpses of their fellows, have simultaneously penetrated one another's cores with lethal shafts of radiation. For a while each has writhed in agony, using his last breath to praise his noble enemy and the noble dance of war. Then death has conquered both.

In other cases, the war has been carried on so vigorously yet so ineffectively that each enemy has actually used up the seemingly inexhaustible springs of his radiation. Each fainting and enfeebled army has been forced to slaughter its own members, one by one, and use their energy for military purposes; until at last the insane and emaciated survivors of each host have even sapped their own vital processes in order to fling a last, impotent but suicidal volley of radiation at the dying foe.

The martial groups were not typical of the social life of the nebulae. They were definitely freaks, whose strange perversion was due to peculiarities in their early history. But though rare, and seemingly doomed to self-destruction, these perverts were to play an important and a baleful part in nebular history.

9. The First Cosmical War

A certain large group of nebulae had long attracted my attention by the unusual breadth and thoroughness of its mental development. Its culture was less exclusively aesthetic than was usual with the nebulae. Intellectual curiosity played an increasingly important part in the life of this group. One party, it is true, sought to concentrate all the interest of the group upon perfecting the physical dance measures of the group, but another was moved chiefly by the will to understand nebular nature and the nature of the universe.

These intellectualists were prone to sacrifice their duties of dance participation to their passion for exploration and experiment. All their experimentation had to be carried on by daring manipulation of their own tissues and was often very painful; but such was their enthusiasm that these nebular scientists were able to discover a good deal about their own biochemical constitution. In spite of much interference and even persecution by the dominant aesthetic party, they were able to construct out of their own tissues optical instruments for the study of the remoter regions of the cosmos, and they obtained in time a clear apprehension of its boundless finitude.

Here at last, I told myself, is the germ of an ampler and a more balanced nebular culture. From this unique group will emerge the idea of a pan-cosmical society of nebulae, a society in which the diversity of all will be a spiritual enrichment to each.

Peering into the dark spaces beyond the confines of their own group, these scientific nebulae discovered, by means of their new instruments, that the innumerable flecks of light observable in all directions were in fact creatures like themselves. Often they longed to go voyaging through these dark populous depths and to make contact with these remote beings. But they knew well that to reach even their nearest neighbors would demand an immense expenditure of power. For although voyaging in the ether is practically unaffected by friction, so that an initial push will propel the traveler for ever, yet only by the use of tremendous energy could he be given sufficient speed to cope with cosmical distances.

Now these nebular scientists learned in time how to unlock the treasury of subatomic energy contained in all matter. But since practically all matter was organized in the living tissues of nebulae, they could not make use of this discovery on a large scale save by sacrificing life. Such a course was repugnant to these highly civilized beings. The members of this group, no matter what their party, had by now conceived a violent dislike even of killing an enemy in battle. Their controversies were by now carried on by methods which the historian would call either more humane or more cowardly according to his taste.

It so happened that this highly cultured group drifted into the proximity of a purely martial group. When these warriors found themselves within striking distance of another community, they composed their own purely fictitious discords in order to unite for the prosecution of the dance measures of war upon a grander scale. With one will they contrived to deflect their orbits sufficiently to bring them actually into contact with the foreign system. Then gleefully they opened battle.

In the more civilized group each party was so deeply opposed to the other, and both were by now so unaccustomed to serious warfare, that resistance was ineffective. Many of the members were killed in the first attack. A belated attempt to use the corpses for the generation of subatomic energy was frustrated by the conquest of the whole group. The invaders became a military caste which sought to impose its barbarian culture upon the combined community.

But peace soon began to undermine the mentality of the invaders. Several of their less disciplined members were infected by the intellectual and aesthetic culture of the enslaved race and were reduced to a state of abject self-loathing by the conflict between their deep-rooted belligerence and the novel ideas which were now germinating within their minds. The leaders therefore determined that a state of war must at once be restored. It seemed at first that, as of old, they would be forced to divide upon some trumpery difference of opinion and organize themselves and their slaves into two armies to fight one another for fighting's sake. But at this point the natural science of the enslaved intelligentsia came to their aid. A cunning and unprincipled intellectual, hoping to better his position in the society, claimed that by the sacrifice of a single life he could provide energy to carry a troop of warriors at a prodigious speed far away into space to attack the nearest foreign groups.

The military caste at once arranged for the slaughter of the most annoying member of the slave race, a sly wit whose overt respectfulness failed to compensate for constant veiled ridicule of war and of the martial temperament. Under the horrified gaze of his fellow intellectuals this nebula was dismembered. A small portion of his flesh was specially treated by the scientist, and then cunningly inserted here and there within the body of a volunteer from the warrior caste. By a secret and subtle method matters were so arranged that the volunteer, by merely exerting his muscles in the ordinary way, should cause the foreign matter to disintegrate and project him rocketwise through space by the rebound of its subatomic energy.

Unfortunately the gallant warrior paid no heed to the cautions of the scientist and exploded his "fuel" too violently at the outset, so that the concussion killed him, and his corpse was hurtled irrevocably into outer space.

This accident roused fury against the scientist. He was seized and tortured, but managed to persuade

the tyrants to give him another chance. Further experiments were undertaken. Finally a speedy but foolproof means of locomotion was achieved, and with it a long-range lethal beam of radiation, which outclassed all former weapons as the machine gun outclasses the spears of savages.

An expeditionary force was now organized. The whole body of the slaughtered slave was divided up amongst these warriors, each of whom was in turn so treated as to have the power of using the stored "fuel."

Thus equipped, the elated army launched itself into space. Its first enterprise called for no hardihood or skill, for it was concerned merely to acquire a huge store of subatomic energy by mopping up a few score of the nearest lone nebulae. Hundreds of these drifted at no very remote distance from the group, like jellyfish in the neighborhood of a shoal of more mobile and more predatory creatures.

Though the army moved at a speed which was regarded as incredible, its voyage lasted a long time even from the point of view of the sluggish nebular consciousness. But it was successful. The unfortunate solitaries, incapable of conceiving what had happened to them, were butchered and cut up into convenient volumes for use as "fuel."

Then followed the first of all imperialistic adventures. The army set out upon a very lengthy voyage to attack the nearest foreign group. This journey took them past many lone nebulae, one or two of which they seized for power. If their aim had been simply exploitation of the economic resources of their neighborhood, the lone nebulae would have contented them. But it was urgent for the warrior race to find a foe before peace undermined them.

Though the size of the expanding cosmos in relation to the size of a nebula or an electron or a lightwave was then very much smaller than it is now, the distance which the little army had to travel in order to reach the nearest foreign community was but a minute fraction of the whole span of the cosmos. And though the speed which they attained was very much faster than the normal drift of nebulae, the impatient warriors found their voyage almost intolerably long and tedious. Before the end of the voyage they fell to quarreling among themselves. Several of them were killed, more were seriously disabled. But the brawl was a tonic to their pugnacious natures, and when at last they reached their destination, they were in extremely good fettle.

The enemy was a large group whose life was almost entirely devoted to the aesthetic expression of personal relationships and the interaction of these with group feeling. Though the defenders outnumbered the attackers by more than five to one, they were of course impotent against the swift movement and long-range "modern" weapons of their enemy. The exultant warriors circled around the doomed aesthetes, pouring into them a concentrated and ceaseless volley of radiation, which "mowed them down" as by machine-gun fire. In a very short time (measured by nebular standards) all semblance of resistance vanished. The survivors floundered among the disorganized corpses of their comrades. Tresses were torn and cast adrift. Cores were pierced, shattered, disintegrated, exploded.

The conquerors proceeded to impose their own martial culture upon the remnants of the group, assuring them that only in the ritual dance of war could true fulfillment of the nebular spirit be attained. Before leaving, they appointed one of their number to carry on the good work of reorganization and enlightened government.

There is no need to tell in detail how the victors returned to their base, improved their method of locomotion and their offensive weapon (by the help of the enslaved intelligentsia), and finally set out, accompanied by the rest of their peers and all the slaves, to conquer and enlighten.

There is no need to tell in detail how they fared. Group after group of nebulae, busy with its own internal strife, or rapt by some endless and subtle terpischorean adventure, or exploring for the first time the mysteries of existence or the depths and heights of personality, found itself attacked by an invincible and ruthless foe, and was speedily overcome.

The policy of the imperialists was to destroy only those communities which refused to accept the imperial law and culture. To those which were amenable they permitted life and a certain autonomy within the bonds of empire. To those which were both sympathetic to their aims and at the same time of warlike temperament they offered partnership within the empire.

For by now the imperialists were opposed not merely by isolated and unarmed groups but by a great alliance of groups equipped with modern weapons and transport. (The enslaved scientists had apparently divulged to the enemy the secret of subatomic power.) It was not with regret but with glee that the imperialists at last found themselves opposed by a worthy foe, and began to organize a vast army picked from among their more warlike vassals and officered by themselves.

The check to imperial expansion was brief. The enemy was a medley of very diverse and unmartial groups united only by a common danger. Stage by stage they were overcome, to be slaughtered or enslaved according to the whim of the victors. Not till a considerable tract of the cosmos had come under the imperial sway did the advancing tide of conquest suffer a check, partly through strife within the empire, partly through the increasing resolution of the resistance.

The cosmos was now like an oyster containing a minute pearl built around an irritating foreign body; for around the empire lay a vaster no-man's-land of perennial warfare, and beyond this again the organized bases of the enemy.

In all these regions the impotent lone nebulae were seized and slaughtered wholesale by both armies for use as power. The strength of the allies was practically inexhaustible. They had the whole cosmos to draw upon, or so much of it as was not too remote to feel the danger or to be brought into action. Behind their front lines rumor of the imperialist danger crept in all directions upon the ether. Translated from language to language, it percolated from remote to ever remoter groups upon the swift-slow rays of cosmical light.

The imperlialists, on the other hand, were already being forced to conserve their resources.

The little band of raiders which had originally

ignited this huge martial conflagration was now a mere handful. Most had either died in battle or succumbed to assassins; for as time passed there was a great increase of discontent among the subject populations. But though the founders of empire were few and hard-pressed, they were still masters of the whole military organization, and they still hoped that at any moment the imperial forces might break the enemy line and overrun a great tract where the lone nebulae drifted in huge shoals awaiting exploitation.

But the great day never came. The imperialists had to decree that each group within the empire should kill one of its members as a source of power for the army. In spite of careful propaganda in praise of dying for the empire, it proved extremely difficult to enforce this order; and when the power which it did provide had been squandered on a huge but barren offensive, the authorities had to demand a second and then a third victim.

The result of the third order was immediate widespread revolt and the downfall of the empire. The unsupported armies, themselves utterly tired and disillusioned, fell back in disorder. The enemy flooded in on all sides, slaughtering the fugitives and making fair promises to the rebels. A ruinous peace was agreed upon perforce by the several revolutionary succession states. The whole war area, and regions far beyond it, resounded with thanksgiving for the end of war and with praise of brotherhood and of the inoffensive life of dance and song and pure intelligence.

But this rejoicing concluded only the first and local

phase of the First Cosmical War. For no sooner was peace declared than the victors, habituated now to all manner of savage passions, to fear, hate, vengeance, and above all to economic greed, began to fight among themselves, and to build up new empires, threading the whole cosmos with the opposed meshes of their alliances.

It would be tedious and unnecessarily harrowing to describe in detail this darkest age of nebular history. Everywhere I "heard" familiar cries, though in nonhuman speech. "Civilization in danger! The war to end war! Wars will never end; you cannot change nebular nature. Reduction of armaments is impracticable. Peace, with security." Everywhere I saw the fair nebular forms mutilated, dismembered, annihilated for power. Everywhere I felt the agony and spiritual stultification of war. Aesthetic activity was everywhere coarsened, partly by the direct influence of martial rhythms and martial sentiments, partly by sheer neglect of the genuine aesthetic experience. The dance life of the average group, even during times of peace, became a barren ritual significant of a past world, meaningless in the present world of war. The life of intellect was stultified by hates and fears, stifled by the endless emergencies of war.

There was of course an increasing awareness of the folly and baseness of war, and an increasing though ill-directed will for peace. Every army now claimed that it fought for peace and a new world order. Every upstart warlord posed as a militant messiah. Gestures of forlorn pacifism became more and more frequent. Individuals and even whole tribes declared that they would fight no more and never again defend themselves. But when it came to the point either their courage failed them, and they took the accustomed course, or some hard-pressed general had them slaughtered for ammunition.

During a lull in the brawling a Pan-Cosmical League was formed to settle all future disputes between rival powers, and to work out a body of principles to guide their conduct toward one another. This league, which claimed to represent public opinion throughout the cosmos, and counted among its members many former enemies, undertook to enforce its judgments if necessary by punitive expeditions and to suppress all unauthorized warfare.

The League maintained a precarious but on the whole beneficial existence, until at last a brigand empire, breaking all its pledges, overran a neighboring tract of unorganized groups. Its conduct was formally condemned by the league; but the powers which it represented took no action. This incident had a significance all too obvious. One by one the most powerful members of the league took to arms in aggressive self-defense. Very soon the cosmical war, which had been reduced to a sporadic brawling between the least civilized communities, blazed up once more.

And what was it all about, this universal slaughter? The constant source of discord was exploitation of the lone nebulae. Each empire was determined to control as large as possible a tract of these inoffensive yet baleful creatures, and to prevent its neighbors from competing with it. For each empire was by now controlled by a small military party which saw in the clash of empires the supreme terpsichorean goal of nebular existence. The mass of unmilitaristic nebulae believed what they were told, namely that for safety against jealous neighbors they must at all costs maintain large reservoirs of power. Thus it was that the nebulae, though beings who were by nature exempt from economic necessity, were trapped into the lust of a power which was useless to them save for mutual destruction. Could anything, I asked myself, be more mad, more barren, more tragically incompetent than this trumped-up greed and mutual fear? But then I remembered my own world.

10. Bright Heart

A new fact, a new movement of the spirit, now emerged in the cosmical drama. It was a twofold and sometimes a self-contradictory movement; and one which, though unique and nebular, was strangely reminiscent of human history. It was one of those great reorientations which are preceded by prolonged chaos and bewilderment. Needs already widespread in the community, and here and there obscurely recognized, remain unfulfilled until they are lived through and expressed and heroically served by a single person of supreme vision and courage. In this case there were two persons, very different in temperament and behavior, but at heart one.

Of these two great ones, the first to make himself felt was originally a member of a small, isolated and youthful group which had for long escaped the ravages of war, but was at last overrun and broken up by a campaign in which its members had no interest whatever. Most of the members were killed or maimed. The dance life of the little community was destroyed. It had been a singularly idyllic community, in which, though the members had matured in a rather loose social order, and had achieved great diversity of self-expression, they were held together in spirit by vivid personal intercourse. Because of their own happy past and the unusual depth of consciousness which they had already achieved, the survivors of the disaster experienced perhaps more poignantly than others the spiritual devastation of the cosmos.

One of these survivors was known to his fellows, and later to the whole cosmos, by a name which can best be translated "Bright Heart." Though this name was given because in his case the nebular core attained an unusual brilliance, it turned out also to be appropriate in a more significant sense.

After the destruction of his community, Bright Heart, wounded but not seriously crippled, set out on a laborious journey through the corpse-strewn war area. Stage by stage, and often on the point of being seized by one army or the other, he crept away (without mechanical aid) into a neighboring "desert" people only by a few lone nebulae. Here for a while he remained, healing his wounds, bitterly grieving for his slaughtered friends, but above all wrestling in his own mind with the problems of his world.

Now it so happened that in his neighborhood two of the lone nebulae drifted within close range of one another and became a binary system, each seemingly destined to distort and wound the other for ever after.

With infinite care and tact, Bright Heart managed to induce each agonized mind to conceive that it was not alone in the universe. And since by good luck neither of the solitaries was yet a mature and rigidly self-sufficient organism, he was actually able to kindle in each a bewildered and excited interest in the other and in himself. With infinite patience he taught these two blind beings to see one another, though obscurely, to talk to one another, and above all so to adjust their internal economy that henceforth the proximity of other conscious beings should no longer be a torture but a joy, a stimulus releasing all manner of new delectable activities of body and mind.

To me, who knew well the absolute solipsism of the lone nebulae, it seemed indeed a miracle that through the insight and faith of Bright Heart these three beings should have been formed into a trinity of lovers. For so it was. With incredulity, and then with awe, I watched their orbits interweave, their tresses lightly trend toward one another and withdraw, or delicately touch and part, fulfilling the rhythms of their new dance life. With amazement I experienced in each of the two emancipated minds first the horror and fury of mutual realization, then, stage by stage under the unerring touch of Bright Heart, mutual interest and mutual need. With grave wonder, too, I experienced through these minds the long ardent story which Bright Heart chanted to them during the dance, the story of the great nebular world with all its horror and its hope, the story of his own heart searchings, and of the purpose which was now clearly forming in his mind.

Only for a short while was this personal beatitude allowed to continue. Presently Bright Heart withdrew, little by little, further and further from his companions, gently reshaping their orbits into a binary system, wistfully bidding them for a while to live on without him in mutual delight and in pursuit of a common aesthetic form. Thus, he said, they must prepare their spirits for the great work which he would later require of them, namely to seek communication with other lone nebulae by means of radio messages, and to awaken them from their solipsism. Thus would the gospel of community, passed from solitary to solitary, percolate throughout the cosmos, until all nebulae, solitary and social alike, would be eager to play their parts in the all-embracing dance pattern of the cosmos. Meanwhile he himself must leave them, to go once more among the social nebulae, preaching the gospel and persuading all to will the end of war.

Withdrawn now from effective gravitational contact with his companions, he still called to them enheartening messages, until they lay beyond the range of his "voice."

For a while the couple carried out faithfully the discipline which Bright Heart had imposed on them. But presently they began to disagree about the interpretation of his teaching, and about their several functions in the immediate dance and in the missionary work which was to come. The quarrel grew bitter, each claiming that he alone was faithful to the spirit of the master. Infuriated with one another, they grappled. The struggle became desperate. The weaker was mangled into insanity. The stronger floated off in proud but guilty self-absorption, seeking in vain to return into solipsistic bliss. Eventually he was butchered for ammunition.

Bright Heart meanwhile had journeyed back among the social nebulae.

Throughout the "modernized" area, which comprised perhaps a third of the cosmos, things were going from bad to worse. War was perennial. Moreover whole populations were now employed in preparing the flesh of the slaughtered for use as "fuel." Innumerable natural groups had been broken up and their members herded together with vast labor corps. Deprived of their natural dance life, and goaded either by force or by propaganda into working themselves beyond their capacity of endurance, they fell sick in body and mind, and died in hundreds.

To these industrial slaves and to the embattled armies themselves Bright Heart now addressed himself. He could not travel far among them, unaided by mechanical power, but he testified fervently to those near at hand, and these spread the gospel. To me it was a gospel at once familiar and strange.

He told of his experience with the two lone nebulae, how they had at first blindly wounded one another, how through his intervention they had become aware of one another, how the discovery had first outraged, then exalted them, how in cooperation they had achieved what was for them a new order of dance life, how in that new life they had found insight into one another and themselves, and had discovered the underlying principle which moved all things. This principle he called by a word which I hesitate to translate—*love*—though I can find no other word for it. Literally its significance was "glad beholding and glad dancing with." Only in "glad beholding and dancing with" one another, he said, could nebulae find peace; and even so, only if they could "gladly behold and dance with" the underlying principle itself. Those who did this could not but long to "gladly behold and dance with" every nebula, could not but strive to turn the cosmos into one great pattern of "glad beholding and dancing," in which every nebula would be enriched by the dance life of all, and each would contribute his unique beauty to the whole cosmical figure.

All this, he said, the two humble solitaries had seen; and now (so he believed) they were ardently preparing themselves for the great mission with which he had charged them, the salvation of their fellows.

He spoke with an eloquence and passion which it is beyond my power to translate into human speech. All I can do is to indicate the bare outline of his theme.

"Is it not true," he said, "that one and all we desire in our hearts above everything else to behold one another gladly, to delight in the endless variety and beauty of one another, and to dance with one another in such rhythms as beauty shall dictate, so that we may be possessed ever more and more by the spirit of glad beholding and dancing? But what beauty are we making? The perfect flesh of the lone nebulae we tear to pieces for power to destroy our fellows. And this violated flesh has poisoned our hearts, with meat for the greed of power and for the fear of one another's greed, so that there is no glad beholding in us, and all our dance is base. Greed and fear are native to us, but in the heart that is possessed by the spirit of glad beholding and dancing they cannot flourish. Then what must we do? We must do always as the spirit dictates, never as greed and fear suggest. We must stop warring. We must give up mechanical power, which is impossible without slaughter of the innocent. And above all, we must look toward one another gladly, even with enemies we must be eager to dance gladly, to express the spirit with them. And if the rulers try to compel us to fight and to use power, we must refuse, even though they punish us with death."

Thus he spoke, urging his ever-increasing followers to live and die for the faith. In season and out of season they must tell the good tidings and exemplify the new way of life. Never must they fight, but they must have the courage of the boldest warrior, and they must welcome death in the cause.

Almost with the speed of light the gospel spread from nebula to nebula. The maimed and the oppressed welcomed it. The mighty at first scorned it and ridiculed it; but when they found that it was a power in the world, they began to deal ruthlessly with the believers. Yet the faith spread. Whole armies were infected by it and refused to fight. Whole populations allowed themselves to be overrun and decimated without resistance.

Such was the success of the movement that the rulers of the warring empires secretly consulted one another as to the best method of checking this universal rot in the morale of their peoples. It was decided that the best plan would be accept the faith and turn it to good use. One by one the lords of the empire announced their conversion. Persecution

ceased. The lieutenants of Bright Heart found themselves treated with respect, and even taken into the
counsel of the governors. Under the influence of
flattery and sympathetic treatment, they began to
see the necessity of compromise. Wild idealism, they
told one another, was ineffective or dangerous. Not
at a leap, but step by step, the millennium must be
reached. The lives of the faithful must not be risked
by unilateral disarmament. Diplomacy must aid
idealism by a realistic search for security. Stage-by-
stage disarmament must be achieved, and deme-
chanization; but not suddenly. The whole social order was at present adapted to warfare and to
mechanical power. A violent change would wreck it.
The office of Bright Heart had been to inspire, and
his work had been nobly done. But the time had now
come for sober practical work, and for that he was
unfit.

Many of the lieutenants of Bright Heart were
hoodwinked by this policy. Under their influence
conditions were made easier for the faithful; but the
faith waned.

11. Bright Heart and Fire Bolt

Bright Heart, in grave perplexity at the turn which events had taken, retired into solitude for a brief spell of meditation and heart searching. It became clear to him that the example which he had set was not enough to grip the simple and inconstant spirits of his followers. He had lived wholly and joyfully according to the faith, but now it was time for him to die for the faith, and in such a manner that his death should set all hearts ablaze.

While he was thus meditating, he was visited by the other greatest mind of the early cosmos. The visitor was a being of a very different kind from Bright Heart. By origin a satellite nebula, he was minute and bald and extremely mobile. But it should be remembered that, though in the nebular view a dwarf, according to our standards he was nevertheless immense. In the normal course of evolution he would end his life by disintegrating into a "globular cluster" of many million stars. At the time of this momentous visit he was still in full maturity and appeared as a bright and definite globe very much smaller than the smallest of nebular cores. His tresses had long since been attracted from him by the mighty central member of his group, around whom he had impotently revolved throughout his bitter youth. Not until the use of subatomic energy had become general had he broken away from that oppressive home life to range about the cosmos at unheard-of speed, replenishing his resources now and then by slaughtering a lone nebula, chastising many a haughty bully, eluding in every region the recruiting sergeants and all those officials who sought to seize him as vagabond, as outlaw, an antimilitary brigand, a disturber of the peace. His success in avoiding capture had depended partly on his extraordinary agility in the use of subatomic energy, partly on his small size; for he was a difficult target, could easily hide among the tresses of a friendly normal nebula, and at no very great distance was invisible to nebular sight.

This unique being bore a name which in his native speech had approximately the significance of the English "Fire Bolt."

To the earnestly meditating Bright Heart now came Fire Bolt, a meteor out of the darkness. The larger nebula, rapt in thought, aimlessly drifted and rotated, as do all nebulae in inaction. His outermost tresses were gathered in upon themselves, imperceiving, inert. Fire Bolt spun round him shouting ethereal halloes to the abstracted spirit of his companion.

At last Bright Heart was roused. He greeted his small visitor with formal, even reluctant politeness; for his meditations were not yet brought to a conclusion. But very soon he was drawn into earnest parley. So lengthy and so vital was the discussion, that the two incongruous beings entered together unwittingly into a unique dance measure, expressing their varying accord and disaccord by inflection of gesture and orbit.

Fire Bolt began by very respectfully expressing his admiration of Bright Heart's work and his acceptance of Bright Heart's aim, namely the creation of the one harmonious and all-embracing dance community in which every nebula should gain fullness of life by faithful participation in the whole cosmical pattern of dance. This, he said, was his own constant aim.

Bright Heart said, "Fullness of life demands not only service in the cosmical pattern but glad beholding of each neighbor as an individual spirit. And this must come first."

"It is true," said Fire Bolt. "It is the chief truth of all. But there are some, the warlords and oppressors, whom, though we must behold them gladly as factors in the universe, we must resist and kill as malefactors in our society. As we must freely give our own lives in service of the neighbors and of the cosmical dance, so we must be ready also to kill in that service."

But Bright Heart said, "That we must never do. That is the great false step, shattering to the dance. Till we are ready in our thousands to die yet never kill, the killers will thrive. Meet evil always with good. Behold all nebulae gladly, even tyrants and hooligans. Expect, and they will dance."

Then Fire Bolt: "In youth, as you can see by my baldness, I was a satellite. My great bully showed me nothing good, nothing worthy to dance with. And as for these warlords and powerlords, they are past savings."

To this Bright Heart replied, "No one is past saving. The underlying principle of glad beholding is in each one of us, striving for expression. That great principle, that spirit which conceived the cosmos, demands that all shall participate."

Again there was a pause, then Fire Bolt said, "I have come to persuade you that though your aim is right and glorious, your method is futile. It would be the right method if nebulae were far more intelligent than they are or far more generous. But in the world that is, not killing but limp mildness is the great error. And what has happened to your work? Triumphant at first, it is now stultified by mildness, and the cunning of the rulers. The time is come for ruthless action. If you will consent, and call your followers to arms, I, who am not without experience of action and not without followers, will be your ally. You shall provide the vision. I will provide the ruthlessness in pursuit of the vision. Together, we can make the new world."

But Bright Heart would not agree. He said only, "No, I will not kill, but I will be killed. And the manner of my dying shall kindle such a spirit as shall never be extinguished."

In vain Fire Bolt pleaded with him. "Can you not see," he said, "that we are all directed by the sheer mechanism of our nature, that we are the sport of mighty forces, that you cannot alter the current of history by a fine example and a momentary widespread glow of emotion? The warlords and power-fiends cannot change their nature. They *must* love mastery, even as I do and you do. And fate has given them a mastery baleful to the people. They are but instruments through which mechanical power enslaves us all. It is useless to appeal to them. We must seize their power. This baleful-precious mechanical power must be controlled by those who will to establish the new world."

"This mechanical power," said Bright Heart, "is to be had only by the slaughter of innocents. The dance pattern of the cosmos needs the cooperation of the lone nebulae no less than ourselves. We must forego power forever."

Fire Bolt answered, "We who are ready to die for the cause must dare to kill. Even when the revolution is achieved, and there is no further need for armaments, we shall still need power, that the lives of citizens may be enriched by swift travel and a thousand joy-giving inventions. Of what use are cattle save for the support of citizens?"

The tresses of Bright Heart quivered and contorted in protest and indignation. But he said only, "Two solitaries I have known, and I have danced long and gladly with them. They are not cattle. They are imprisoned in themselves, but they shall be set free."

There was a pause, then Fire Bolt said, "I find it in my heart to believe you, and indeed you may well be right. It may be that the new world, when it has been established, will forego power and emancipate the lone nebulae. But meanwhile we must use them, or the revolution will never be achieved."

For some while, Bright Heart and Fire Bolt continued to plead with one another, but neither was convinced. Finally it was agreed that Bright Heart should first carry out his new plan, challenging the rulers even to the point of martyrdom; but that, if his death failed to bring in the new world, Fire Bolt should let loose his revolution.

12. Death of Bright Heart

Slowly, unaided by mechanical power, Bright Heart returned to the busy and unhappy region whence he had come. With all his strength he broadcast his challenge to the rulers, and to their minions, his own tricked followers.

To the disheartened faithful in all that region he cried, "Away with lying compromise! Refuse, refuse to do the foolish and wicked things that the rulers make to seem prudent and honorable. Refuse in your thousands, and all their power will vanish. They will kill us. Let them kill us by hundreds and thousands. But they cannot kill us all. There will be enough left for the making of the new world. Let us die gladly for the new world."

The authorities made haste to seize Bright Heart. But his words were already abroad upon the ether, and could not be recalled. So they tortured him to force him to recant what he had said. But he continued to proclaim the truth. When he was at the point of death he cried out, "Look! Look! The great Maker who made all nebulae in his likeness watches us from outside the world. His heart is bright. His tresses can brace the cosmos."

I, myself, half expecting to see a divine eternal nebula beyond the hosts of mortal nebula, looked. It was a strange shock to me to see, peering through the veil of innumerable nebulae, the almost human face of God, remote, inscrutable, intent, kindled (as it seemed to me) to ecstasy by the creatures of his own artistry.

Looking once more to Bright Heart, I saw that he was dead, and that slaves were taking his flesh to the nearest munition makers.

But the manner of his death and the words that he had spoken were rumored from empire to empire throughout the cosmos. And it was said that he himself was the bright-hearted God, and that he had come into the world to save nebulae from their own folly.

Everywhere it was said, "Let us set up the new world now without delay, before we forget the glory of this death." Munition slaves left their batalions in hundreds to join the peace army of Bright Heart's followers. Warriors broke up the dance life of their regiments and foreswore their weapons, fraternizing with the enemy. Empires were shaken and over-thrown by the tidal wave of the new life which advanced in all directions like the tremors of an earthquake.

Fire Bolt, observing these great events, wondered whether after all Bright Heart had been right and the new world was to be without further agony.

But presently he saw that, though many rulers had fallen, their places had been taken by others of the same kind, who, while they spoke fair to Bright Heart's followers, established themselves by the old methods. Then one by one the rulers told their peoples that some neighboring power was insincere in its protestations of goodwill and was secretly planning an attack. Secretly each government provided its neighbors with evidence of its own warlike intentions, for use as propaganda. Thus, as the passion caused by Bright Heart's death waned, and became only a memory, the peoples were tricked once more into fear and hate and war. And the priestly leaders of the followers of Bright Heart told their respective peoples that the divine spirit of Bright Heart, the underlying principle of glad beholding and dancing, was bidding them wage the last of all wars to clear the cosmos of the evil-minded foe.

13. Fire Bolt

Fire Bolt, after his talk with Bright Heart, had retired to his own much harassed region; and there he had set about inspiring and training a picked band of followers.

He said to them, "We are the instruments of fate. Our wills are the expression of mighty forces at work in the cosmos. Through us the new world will be founded. Hitherto, power has been with the masters, the oppressors. Inevitably they have exercised it in their own interests, not for the world. But now, power is no longer in their hands alone. The knowledge of mechanical power, the skill for using it, has passed to those whom the oppressors enslaved. They have only to will resolutely to overthrow the oppressors and create the new world. If they will it, it will happen; for power is theirs. And it is for us who do will it, and do understand the way in which fate is working, to show the oppressed their opportunity and lead them to victory."

This he said in season and out of season. And he kindled his followers with his own fire, and he trained them secretly in the technique of obtaining mechanical power from disintegrating nebular flesh, and in the use of it for locomotion and offense.

While he was doing this, he watched the career of Bright Heart. And when Bright Heart died, Fire Bolt said to his followers, "If we were all like him, there would be no need for revolution. Let us wait and see whether the example of his life changes the wills of nebulae, and brings the new world peaceably, as he hoped. It will not; but let us have proof that it will not, so that we may convince the oppressed peoples that there is nothing for it but to destroy their oppressors."

And when at last the oppressors had tricked the followers of Bright Heart, and the empires were once more at war, and the peoples were everywhere slaving to produce power or to defeat an enemy people, Fire Bolt sent his followers abroad to create more and ever more followers, until in every group, in every munition corps, in every troop of warriors, there was a follower of Fire Bolt, working for the revolution, stirring up discontent, whispering seditious truths, appointing to each convert a particular task in the worldwide preparation and in the worldwide revolution itself.

When all was ready, Fire Bolt gave the signal. Slowly it spread abroad upon the ethereal undulations from nebula to nebula. And as it passed, the conflagration which had been so carefully planned leapt into life. One by one, and with surprisingly little fighting, the peoples came into their own.

But the revolution did not spread throughout the cosmos. The remoter regions had not been well enough prepared. In some the people rose too late to surprise the masters, and after a desperate struggle were subdued. In some they were half-hearted, or did not rise at all. Rather less than a third of the population of the cosmos was set free by the revolution.

The peoples that had freed themselves now set about reorganizing their society, under the leadership of Fire Bolt. It was widely hoped that each nebula would now be allowed to go back to his native group and find full expression in the dance life of the group. For there was a widespread desire to express in significant dance forms all the cumulative passion of revolution. Many said to Fire Bolt, "Help us now at last to work out and establish the first measure of the cosmical dance pattern."

But Fire Bolt said, "The enemy outnumbers us by two to one, and will surely attack us. We must prepare for a very desperate war. But we shall win, and we shall free the enemy peoples, for we shall be strengthened by our great cause."

So the freed peoples freely submitted themselves to a very strict discipline. While there was yet time they drilled and practiced all the undertakings of war, and they piled up ammunition. And the enemy, seeing this, hastened their preparations. And the enemy rulers told their peoples that the revolutionary peoples had fallen into a worse servitude than before, that they were being cunningly and brutally used by their tyrants, that all glad beholding and dancing had vanished from them, and that Bright Heart, who watched from his heaven outside the cosmos, commanded all true believers to join together for the overthrow of that evil society.

The war which followed was lengthy and destructive; but, though outnumbered, the peoples of the revolution were in the end victorious. For they had faith, unity of purpose and Fire Bolt. One by one the enemy peoples either suffered defeat, or spontaneously broke out into revolution.

When the war was over, and all social nebulae throughout the cosmos had entered the revolutionary society as free citizens, everyone agreed that it was time to establish the cosmical dance pattern of all nebulae, which alone could afford every nebula the deepest aesthetic satisfaction, and was indeed the whole goal of nebular existence.

Innumerable voices enquired of Fire Bolt how this thing was to be done. Now Fire Bolt was no longer what he had once been. He had used himself up in the revolution, and he was desperately tired. Moreover a strange "crumbling disease" was beginning to attack him, a disease increasingly common among the minute "satellite" nebulae, and by now not wholly unknown among the normal nebulae. His outer tissues were disintegrating into minute dense grains of fiery gas, and where this had happened his flesh was as though it was no longer his own. He could not move it. He could not perceive with it. Fire Bolt, in fact, was growing old. He was beginning to pass over from being a nebula to being a globular cluster of stars, a minute galaxy. But inwardly he was still almost his old ardent self, though tired, utterly tired.

Now there were two views as to the kind of thing the cosmical dance pattern should be. According to one party it should be stately and restrained; and the

course of each nebula should lie wholly within his own group. The cosmos should become a lovely pattern of distinct minuet figures. According to the other much larger party the cosmic dance must be far more violent. It must symbolize and commemorate by its far-flung measures the conflicts and agonies of the past. Only by an extravagance of swift intricate movement could it by potent suggestiveness waken the nebulae to a new order of percipience, intelligence and creative power. Moreover it was hoped that from the ecstasy born in every heart by means of this superb communal activity there might emerge an oversoul or single spirit of the cosmos, in whose exalted experience every individual nebula should participate.

Now the less violent dance program could be carried out wholly by means of the native energies of the dancers, but the other entailed a huge expenditure of mechanical power. This would have to be obtained, as formerly, by the sacrifice of the lone nebulae, for there was no other source of energy but the flesh of the nebulae themselves. The advocates of the less violent dance insisted that the office of the lone nebulae could not be merely to give their lives for fuel but to play their part consciously and joyfully in the dance. No cosmical dance pattern could be wholesome, or significant, or satisfying to any sensitive individual, if the greater part of the cosmical population had to be left out of it entirely and murdered for its support. Those world citizens who still accepted the teaching of Bright Heart dared to point out that their master had actually succeeded in awakening two of the lone nebulae to a sense of

community. Surely it was a supreme duty to organize a worldwide mission to the lone nebulae, so as to
emancipate them from their solipsistic prison cells,
and kindle them with the gospel of community, and
the holy zest of the cosmical dance.

But the other party would have none of this. They
declared that the lone nebulae were mere brutes,
cattle to be used up as seemed fitting to the community. The only right which could be claimed for them
was the right to humane slaughter. All agreed that
the supreme goal of existence was the creation of the
cosmical dance pattern. After all then it was a
kindness to the lone nebulae to enable them to
contribute something important toward this end in
the only way which was possible to them, namely by
yielding up their flesh for fuel. Confident in their
numbers and their realism, this party appealed to
Fire Bolt to exercise his presidential fiat and forbid
their opponents to disturb the harmony of the great
cosmical undertaking by advocating their idealistic
yet cowardly policy. Thinking to rouse his jealousy
they added a suggestion that this heresy was a
symptom of the widespread resurrection of the impracticable and sentimental ideals of Bright Heart.

But Fire Bolt, already fatigued by the effort of
"listening" to their lengthy petition, replied in a
manner wholly unexpected. "That great seer," he
said, "erred only in having too good an opinion of
nebular nature. He underestimated the weakness
and stupidity of the peoples, and the self-regard of
the oppressors. He thought the new world would be
brought into being by the good will of all, not by the
hate and courage of a few. But at bottom he was

right. Though to overthrow the oppressors we had to do many terrible things and sacrifice many social and many lone nebulae, now that we have freed the world we must 'gladly behold' *all* nebulae, and dance with *all* nebulae, sacrificing none. I am sick and dying. You will remember me, for without me you could not have made the revolution. But more earnestly, more constantly, remember Bright Heart. For his work is still for you to do."

The petitioners departed in indignation, murmuring, "His mind is going." They tried hard to keep Fire Bolt's pronouncement from being made known, but the old sick nebula gathered his strength together to force his dying flesh to one last effort. One last, long impassioned speech he made, condemning the aims of the majority, pleading for the lone nebulae and for the unmechanized dance, and praising Bright Heart. Before he had said all that was in his mind to say, his speech organs were paralyzed.

Not long afterward he lost all power of movement and of external perception. He became as one of the lone nebulae, though rich in precious memories of intercourse, memories of Bright Heart, of sedition, of revolution, and of the new world which he had founded. For a while his old spirit flickered on, imprisoned within an unresponsive dust of stars. And then he died.

But his last appeal spread slowly, irresistibly, upon the ethereal medium, and was passed on from nebula to nebula.

14. The Last Phase
of the Nebular Era

The party which stood for the more primitive
dance and for the emancipation of the lone nebulae
was greatly strengthened by the dying speech of Fire
Bolt, for the prestige of the great revolutionary was
at its height. But most nebulae, and almost all who
were in authority, continued to favor the policy of
the mechanized cosmical dance life. The delight in
the power and freedom of mechanical locomotion
was by now too deeply rooted to be easily foresworn.
The government, moreover, saw in the more violent
dance a far greater scope for governmental control
and centralization than in the other.

While the dispute was raging it was suggested
that no important decision should be made till experiment had revealed the actual capacities of the lone
nebulae to respond to educative influence. Some of
the party which advocated the more primitive dance
life therefore set about making contact with several
of the lone nebulae. They very soon found that the
task was far more difficult than they had expected.
Not one of them had Bright Heart's genius for sympathetic insight and tact. Their clumsy efforts to

give the solitaries an inkling of their presence were at first entirely unsuccessful. When, later, they managed to develop a partially successful technique, they received an unpleasant surprise. The lonely mind to whom they had with such difficulty revealed themselves had been so mauled and infuriated by their efforts that he regarded the intruders with furious hate, and would do nothing but stab blindly at them with shafts of his native radiation. Even when the technique had been so far improved that mental intercourse could be achieved without distressing the solitary, the attempt to give him some idea of the external world, by speech and by training his rudimentary powers of external vision, generally put him to such a severe mental strain that he had a nervous breakdown. In many cases the unfortunate patient went mad.

Nevertheless the missionaries persevered, and in time they succeeded in producing about a score of "enlightened" lone nebulae, capable of external perception, of speech and of locomotion.

The curious flocked in from every side to meet these emancipated savages; and the solitaries themselves were eager to learn as much as possible (in small doses) of the amazing world into which they had so unexpectedly been flung.

After a while it became clear that the various individual lone nebulae were reacting to their new environment in very different ways. Those that were relatively backward in physical and mental development not only adapted themselves comparatively easily to the life which was going on around them, but declared that in glad beholding and glad dancing with other individuals, especially with one or two intimate friends, they discovered a new joy, and one which was altogether more delectable than any familiar joys. Some went even so far as to say that their earlier life had been obscured by a vague sense of frustration and futility which now at last had given place to bliss. They asked only to be allowed to live the life of personal love undisturbed forever, expressing their inner ecstasy in mystic love dance now with one individual now with another, or with twos and threes, as the spirit moved them.

But the more developed nebulae reacted in a very different manner. The goal of life for every nebula, they said, must ever be to awaken the spirit so far as possible in percipience, intelligence and appreciation. This could be done only by the life of dance action, external or internal. It was true that by the external behavior of many nebulae acting in relation to one another the dance was made capable of far greater complexity; but, they affirmed, it was made no more significant. What had these proud but brutish social nebulae really achieved by their vaunted social life? They talked much of glad beholding and dancing, but in truth, instead of dancing in harmony with one another, they had perpetually been in conflict. Each was a curse to his neighbors, and none had been able to attain more than the crudest and most superficial aesthetic perception. Their finer perceptions had been stifled under the urgent need to defend themselves against one another. The hurly burly of social life had deprived them of inner reality. It was this lack of inner being that had made them so obtuse as to suppose that mechanical locomotion could be used to produce significant dance forms. Could anything more fantastically false be conceived than the notion of *self-*expression by means of power not one's own, and in terms of a violent kind of locomotion intolerable to the true nebular nature? These empty creatures were only of importance because of their harmfulness. Already they had decimated the population of lone nebulae, and unless prevented they would exterminate them. It was evidently necessary to rouse the lone nebulae from their serious life, not to make them permanently social but in order that, by a temporary cooperation, they might destroy the social nebulae.

Among the social nebulae themselves the dispute over the lone nebulae became more and more violent. Each party claimed that the experiment had proved its case. The advocates of mechanical power argued that although a few lone nebulae might, with infinite trouble, be educated to take a humble part in the cosmical dance, the great majority were clearly too far gone in solipsism to appreciate the beauty of communal life. The advocates of the primitive dance, on the other hand, claimed with reason that the lone nebulae were not mere brutes, that they were intelligent and highly aesthetic minds, and that, if only they could be won over for community, their help in the production of a profoundly significant cosmical dance order would be invaluable.

The conflict was irreconcilable. The advocates of mechanical power took matters into their own hands. They seized government, proscribed their opponents and organized a worldwide heresy hunt.

But the party of the primitive dance was not to be so easily crushed. In many regions they were able to paralyze the activities of the government; in one region they were in a majority. There they organized themselves for war and embarked upon a dual policy toward the lone nebulae under their sway. They sent missions among them to rouse them from their solitariness, and gave to the missionaries these instructions. Each lone nebula, when he had been educated into clear awareness of the community, was to be asked whether he wished to participate in the cosmical dance or not. If he was ready to do so, he was to be treated as a citizen; if he refused he was to be slaughtered for power.

The "primitive" party would certainly have been beaten in the struggle which followed, had they not discovered a new weapon, far more destructive than the simple beams of radiation which had hitherto been used. The inventor of the new method of attack was one of the socialized lone nebulae. He was a prince of outspoken cynics, for he had declared that though he cared not a rap for any nebula but himself, he saw the necessity of supporting the "primitives" to save his own life. The end which he desired, he boldly declared, was that all nebulae of every party and type should be destroyed, except himself. But for the present he was willing to help the less dangerous pack of brutes against the more dangerous.

The new weapon consisted of a ray which would not only shatter the enemy but would start in his flesh a process of atomic disintegration so violent that all nebulae in his neighborhood would be infected. He only wished, he said, that he could safely use this weapon on his friends as well as on his enemies.

Not till the enemy population had been halved did they discover a means of checking the spread of this diabolic infection, and at the same time learn to use the deadly ray upon their opponents.

It would be tedious to follow the course of the war, which dragged on indecisively aeon after aeon. Its end was ignominious to both antagonists. Neither triumphed; both were reduced to impotence by forces independent of the enemy.

Throughout the nebular era two slow but irresistible changes, independent but interacting, were setting a limit to the life of any possible cosmical community of nebulae, and to the lives of individual nebulae also. The first of these was the continued expansion of the cosmos, the second was the senescence of the individual nebulae.

Owing to the expansion, it became increasingly difficult to communicate with remote groups. Not only did messages take longer and longer, but also they entailed an ever greater expenditure of energy. Even the concentration of radiation into a beam did not do away with this difficulty; for even the finest beam spread to some extent. Actual locomotion from region to region of the cosmos was still more seriously hampered. Distances were so increasing that, though short trips from neighbor to neighbor were scarcely at all affected, long voyages to other groups were becoming ever more lengthy and costly. The cosmos, in fact, was beginning to disintegrate.

The difficulties due to the expansion would not have been so formidable had the nebulae retained their youth. But senescence was by now making it less possible for them to readjust themselves to changing circumstances. They were becoming more hidebound, more sluggish, less percipient. For by now the "crumbling disease" which had destroyed Fire Bolt was a widespread plague, especially among the social nebulae, whose more active life seems to have worn them out more rapidly than the solitaries.

Nebula after nebula, group after group, munition corps after munition corps, regiment after regiment succumbed to the strange disease. It did not suggest the spread of infection from some particular region. It was endemic in every region, and ever on the increase. At first it had been regarded as a curious and unimportant accident, much as we should regard the case of a man who should have the rare misfortune to choke himself with his own saliva. But as the plague increased, it became a matter for public concern; and in time it grew to be even more momentous than the war itself.

For as the war dragged on, aeon after aeon, now this side securing an advantage, now the other, a larger and larger proportion of the combatants was put out of action by the "crumbling disease." Finally things came to such a pass that war was simply brought to a standstill. Both armies lost heart in the endless campaigns, and melted away. The authorities had not the means, if they had the will, to send them back to the front. A few heroically or fanatically militaristic warriors did indeed struggle to keep up the fray. For a long time it was possible to discover here and there a couple of aged foes still clumsily attacking one another. Purblind, stiff-limbed and mentally enfeebled, they would fumblingly direct their lethal beams at one another; but so palsied and incompetent were they that as often as not they blew up their own bodies instead of striking the enemy.

But most nebulae, as soon as they found their powers decaying, or even earlier, were too depressed to carry on their military duties. They crept away into a quiet place to snatch whatever comfort was possible in their distress, to mumble their store of memories, to lament over their aches and pains, to converse laboriously, like deaf old men, with their aged companions.

Thus one by one these first and hugest of all living things fell into decay. Even now, in our human era, all are not dead. Some, like our own great galaxy, retain a smouldering core, organic and distressfully alive. In this galaxy of ours the vital core is hidden from man by huge clouds of dead and nonluminous matter; but our astronomers have already guessed its existence, though not its vital constitution. Most of the flesh of our once superb and ardent nebula, most of the sensitive and agile organs with which it perceived and created beauty, crumbled long ago into that inconceivably sparse dust of stars which now surrounds us. But the old heart, or rather brain, still maunders on to itself about the glorious and tragic past and about its present blind isolation and misery.

Even in our day a few far-scattered nebulae are still almost untouched by decay. They see around them nothing but the ruins of their world, their dying or their dead companions. They themselves are still alert and sensitive. Like the lone survivor of a shipwreck, each strives to construct for himself a semblance of comfort in the desolation. And since for nebulae the only really satisfying activity is ever the dance, they can but dance to themselves measures symbolic of the ardent past. With subtle rhythms and patterns, they recapture their own lost youth, their loves and hates, their mature ambitions, and all the follies and agonies of the great nebular community. They epitomize and transmute into the language of dance the whole past of their race with all its heroic ventures, its tragically missed opportunities, its conflicting purposes, its horrors and frustrations, its perennial dream of the glad beholding and dancing of every nebula with all others in the never realized cosmical dance life.

But in our day the great majority of the formerly alive and sentient host are already crumbled into stars. Their voluntary movements have long ago ceased. They drift and slowly spin under the influences of gravitation alone. The stars themselves, fiery particles left over from the continuous living tissues, also spin and drift, held loosely together, in the system that we call galaxies, by their combined gravitational influence.

15. Interlude

Watching this universal senescence, this inevitable disruption of the communal life of a whole cosmos, I was oppressed with human pity and with human indignation against the author of a creature at once so full of promise and so futile.

Why, why, I cried in my loneliness, did God endow his cosmos with such wealth of physical power and of spiritual potentiality if the issue was to be nothing but desolation?

For it seemed to me in that long drawn out decline that not merely the nebulae but the cosmos itself had entered into senility, and that any subsequent life or movement of the spirit could only be a dying flicker.

I looked back in memory along the vista of the aeons. As one recollects the earliest recoverable incidents of childhood, I remembered that moment when the atom-cosmos had first responded to God's word and lavished itself in light. I saw once more the teeming, the jostling and agitated host of the newborn nebulae. I recalled that less distant age, when, more scattered and more mature, those eager spiritual adventurers were discovering the true direction of their nature, and exploring, not without disaster,

the strange universe of their dance life. I saw them
at last tricked and led astray by the misuse of
knowledge, squandering their wealth of power and
their strength of spirit on false goals. Not in memory
only but in vivid perception I saw them one and all
dying, their true life unrealized.

I had a curious fantasy that the cosmos was now
like a deserted room, closed up and stifling. From
outside, the sunlight, pouring through shut windows, lit up the lifeless dust motes, hanging in the
air. The curtains never moved. A flower in an empty
vase drooped.

A strange passion of loneliness seized me. Like a
prisoner I could have battered on the walls of the
cosmos, had there been any walls. But I was imprisoned in a boundless finitude. Around me the dust of a
dead world stagnated in the ether.

"Oh God, oh God, let me out," I cried, "or kill me."

I peered beyond the dead hosts of the nebulae.
There, there still, outside the boundless finitude of
the cosmos, God still watched the processes that he
had set in motion.

From the bottom of my being, I loathed him.

The features became clearer. Dread face of power!
Brutish, human, celestial! I strained and strained to
read God's face. But it was inscrutable.

Cruel? Indeed, no! Compassionate? No! Or in a
manner, yes? For surely that calm attentive gaze
meant not mere calmness, mere aloofness. Did it
perhaps mean passion transmuted? Did it speak of
inner participation in all grief and joy? Perhaps. Yet
it was ruthless, as though compassion had been
absorbed and used in some loftier and relentless
exaltation.

Four Encounters

Contents

Introduction
to the British Edition

"Doubt is the offspring of knowledge; the savage never doubts at all." The words are not Olaf Stapledon's, but Winwood Reade's.

Winwood Reade wrote the little-remembered *The Martyrdom of Man,* which was first published in 1872. Among other intellectual pleasures, *The Martyrdom of Man* offers a concise history of the world since the planets first formed round the sun, to "rotate like joints before the fire," and a predictive history of the future. The emphasis it placed on Process was novel and alarming.

Among Reade's audience was H. G. Wells, who declared how strongly Reade's book influenced him. Like attracts like, and the far-sighted Stapledon must also have been powerfully moved by Reade's book; originality builds on firm foundations, and Stapledon's greatest works, *Last and First Men* and *Star Maker,* must owe an honorable debt to Reade's intoxicating mixture of fact and speculation.

If doubt is the offspring of knowledge, then this book is the offspring of doubt. Although *Four Encounters* may be regarded as operating on a small scale, it covers a wide canvas, the whole canvas of modern questioning.

William Olaf Stapledon would require no introduction were it not that he has suffered from neglect by publishers and critics. He has an ardent following of readers, who will not need my words. Neglect attends any writer who is ahead of his time or stands apart from main literary currents. Jesus' bitter truth about a prophet being not without honor save in his own country is aptly quoted in such circumstances. Comfortable myopia is the enemy of foresight.

In the circumstances, my duty is first of all to say that I find this volume profound and moving, not least in Stapledon's perception that there are many truths, to which different temperaments must remain loyal.

For this is a book of conversations, not conversions. In four dialogues, the Stapledon persona encounters a Christian, a Scientist, a Mystic, and a Revolutionary. Views are aired, often pungently, opinions are not changed. Beside the passion of debate runs the dispassion of enquiry—we recognize both as Stapledonian qualities, although the method is Socratic.

One derives two kinds of pleasure from the book. To begin with, there is a beautiful contrapuntal argument that runs through all four pieces. In the first piece, an embittered engineer finds that belief returns to him when he surveys the interior of a cathedral, wondering at the fact that "stone should live and praise while in our hearts faith lies dead." At the same time, the Stapledon persona makes an unstressed analogy with the universe itself, "the vastness of the physical," and finds peace in the reflection that, if our small grain of a world can harbor spirit, much greater things must be at large in the wholeness, the hugeness, of space and time.

So the persona achieves a plane of thought where thought itself is impotent. Some intimations lie beyond words. For mankind may form one instrument in the orchestra of the universal spirit's music. "Whether this music is only to be appreciated gropingly by the players themselves, or whether it is for the discerning joy of some cosmical artist, or perhaps in some incomprehensible way for the very music itself, we cannot know." Language cannot assist us in resolving the problem, for language is no more than "primitive grunts of a terrestrial animal."

Does Stapledon contradict himself here? Can we be both part of a universal music and little better than grunting animals? We can. The answer is to cease grunting. "Even if I say 'Thou! Oh, Thou!' I say too much."

In the second conversation, the argument with the geneticist runs in different channels, although always with reference to a larger sphere of existence. The geneticist will have no nonsense with the music of the spheres. Other intelligent species may well exist in the universe, but what of them? "They are beyond our reach and I hope we are beyond theirs." The scientist emerges as even more prideful than the Christian; like the latter, and the Mystic, he lives in a partly sought estrangement from his fellow beings, and from love.

Love forms a vivid subtheme in the book. The

Stapledon persona sees love as an agent that has at least the potential to free us from various kinds of self-involvement; whereas each of the four characters against whom he is ranged see it as a web, a net, a seductive distraction.

This attitude is best displayed in the last two conversations. The Mystic puts love away from himself in an attempt to gain self-transcendence. But this may be a trap he falls into while attempting to avoid the snare of sensation; he can no longer care for people. To the Stapledon persona, this is false; people matter as they are manifestations of the spirit.

To my mind, this third conversation is the most seductive and compelling.

But the argument is developed further in the last piece, where the revolutionary-minded mechanic believes—and his girl friend believes even more strongly—that it is society that matters, not individuals. Here the spirit previously talked about so freely is narrowed to exclude all but the corporate entity of the middle or the working class. The Stapledon persona has been willing to accept the validity of spirit as a larger and all-pervasive force; he rejects it in a narrow Marxist connotation. What is under examination here is the whole concept of mankind, now seen as a social unit needing economic salvation, whereas previously it has been presented as individuals striving for individual salvation.

So the argument broadens, narrows, opens out again. In many ways, this last piece is most powerful, not least because the mechanic is divided against himself, and so comes over more clearly as a person, less as a dialectic.

One error of reasoning that Stapledon causes the mechanic to commit is of significance. The mechanic argues that an understanding of historical processes leads to a desire for the happiness of mankind as a whole. This is by no means so. It is more likely to lead to the distancing skepticism of a Gibbon, the disgust of a Swift, the learned *schadenfreude* of a Spengler. No man can be cheered by a study of Byzantium.

But Stapledon does not present us with dismay in his works. With disarray, yes, with a questioning of the Immanent Will that rivals Thomas Hardy's; but never with undiluted pessimism. Indeed the fine conclusion to *Last and First Men,* "it is very good to have been man," is often quoted against Stapledon as an example of smugness. The truth seems to be that Olaf Stapledon was one of the first writers to achieve a true and level agnostic perspective on the processes of history (and beyond history, on the processes of the universe of which we have only just realized we form part). If doubt is honorable, his viewpoint is ultimately the only sane one.

Having said this, I will say by contrast that Stapledon is intensely English in outlook. There is no contradiction here. Shakespeare was not of an age, but for all time; he was also a Warwickshire man. I began by saying that one derived two pleasures from this book. The first pleasure lies in the language; "Thou! Oh, Thou!" may be too much, but many phrases are sufficient unto themselves. Whenever the argument threatens to become diffuse, there is an apothegm to make it all clear. What is more English in its moderation and tone than "Marxism is all very well, but if you push it too far it turns just silly"? And much of Stapledon and his philosophical stance is summed up in "I said I could understand the view that *nothing* mattered, but that society as such should matter, rather than individuals, seemed to me a crazy notion." The combination of lofty idea and common English goes down well.

I have been careful throughout to refer to the "I" character in the four dialogues as "the Stapledon persona." It is always a mistake to charge the "I" character in any fiction with representing exactly the feelings and opinions of its author—a mistake that readers and critics perpetually tumble into. But is *Four Encounters* fiction? Stapledon always took care to remind us that his writings were not prophecy but myth, that what he said would raise thunder "both on the Left and the Right," and that his novels are fictionalized philosophy. In this book the fictionalization is, at first blush, of a small order. Yet there are always touches of a true novelist at hand, glimpses of nature at work of a starling gulping a butterfly, which, though introduced for a didactic end, nevertheless serve to heighten the argument and adorn the tale.

Perhaps it is misleading to suggest, as I have, that the book represents a whole and comes to a well-wrought conclusion. I do perceive such unity, while knowing from the book's history that it is an accidental unity. Perhaps the coherence of the universe is no less unplanned.

A pattern if not a plan emerges from the prehistory of the book. While I was in New York in April of 1975, I was phoned by Harvey Satty, who told me that he had in his possession an unpublished Stapledon manuscript. I was in quest of things American, not things British, but my surprise was the surprise of an explorer of the Mayan civilization who trips across, in the rain-drenched forests of Yucatan, the secret of the Great Pyramid in Egypt.

The manuscript proved to be *Four Encounters*. Mr. Satty told me that Agnes Stapledon, the writer's widow, was willing to have it published if I would write the Introduction to it. This I am now doing, confident that I am unequal to the task. My qualifications, like the coherence of the universe, are accidental. I introduced *Last and First Men* to the Penguin-reading public in 1963, and I devoted a eulogistic section to Stapledon's novels in *Billion Year Spree,* my history of science fiction. I am proud and horrified to appear in a spot that, I feel, should be occupied by someone with philosophical credentials.

Mrs. Stapledon has told me that the exact date of composition of the four pieces is uncertain. Internal evidence—reference to bombed cathedrals in the first and the rudimentary engineering of the vehicle in the fourth—indicates that they must have been written in the second half of the 1940s; which is to say the five years immediately preceding Stapledon's death in 1950.

The plan was, Mrs. Stapledon says, to produce a series of conversations, perhaps as many as ten. These four are all that exist. Who the other conversationalists would have been can only be surmised. I would certainly like to have read of the meetings with a Capitalist, a Sensualist, a Historian, a Doctor, and a Writer—in the expectation that some of them would turn out to be women. Here perhaps is an exercise for the newly formed Stapledon Society.

It remains for me only to say that the arguments have dated very little in the quarter century that has been passed since they were written. The fears and aspirations that Stapledon explores are no ephemeral things. Some topics strike us as remarkably to the point. For instance, as Amnesty International has recently pointed out, torture as a deliberate policy of state is on the increase all over the world. The case for torture is unflinchingly presented here.

People feel guilty about killing and hurting others. That is good because guilt is socially useful. "All the same, in an urgent revolutionary situation it's irrational, it's plain madness, to let our emotional habit of squeamishness endanger the revolution." From Tokyo and Moscow to Sao Paulo and Santiago, such arguments are fashionable. We need our defense against them. In its cool and civilized meditations, this book is an item to be reckoned with in that defense.

Brian W. Aldiss

A Christian

I have met a Christian, and now I must tell you about him; for you are always the touchstone.

He was no typical Christian, nor yet one of outtanding saintliness. He was his unique self, but also a Christian, and to me, arresting.

Sitting in the cathedral, I thought how strange that stone should live and praise, while in ourselves faith lies dead. The columns stand so confidently, joined in their upstretched hands like dancers waiting for the music. They have waited for centuries.

Today, more formidable columns, sudden, fungoid, springing from land and sea, threaten all of us.

In the cathedral choir, masons were repairing war damage. I heard metal strike the stone. The windows were pallid, for the warm glass had all been treasured away. Near me in the knave, two spinsters with guidebooks devoured information. A youth in shorts, a peroxide girl, a bunch of trippers, stared vacantly; sheep lost in a desert. Yet a cathedral is a sheepfold. Or so it was intended.

Presently vergers were shepherding out the sight-

seers; for a service was due, and a mild bell tolling. I
retreated. But as I was nearing the door, the Christian touched me, and said, "You looked unhappy.
Perhaps I might help." My resentment was quiet-
ened by his face, where peace was imposed on some
still restless grief; a face carved heavily, the eyes,
dark holes, dark gleaming wells; the nose a buttress;
the mouth, mettlesome but curbed.

I said, "If I was unhappy, it was for the world, not
for myself." He answered, "The world is indeed un-
bearable; unless we are given strength. Darkness is
everywhere; but there is a light to lighten it." Brutally I said (for you were not with me to temper me),
"You want to add me to your converts, but my scalp
is not for your belt." His hand reached toward me but
withdrew. He turned to leave me. Ashamed, I said,
"Oh, forgive me! Please come with me and tell me
about your light."

But even as I spoke, there flashed on me a memory. I was a freshman returning to Oxford by train,
reading in my corner. A godly woman opposite me
laid a hand on my knee. "Are you saved?" she said.
Startled and crimson, I answered, "No! At least I
don't think so. But I don't think I want to be. Thank
you all the same." With knit brows, I stared at my
book, incapable of reading.

And now, half a lifetime later, here was I asking
this other Christian to tell me about his light. We
emerged from the cathedral into the sunshine and
the town's roar. Beyond the lawns of the close, how
the shops, banks, hotels impended! As though a lava

flood had been by miracle congealed to save God's house.

We paced, and neither spoke.

Presently, he said, sighing, "I was obtuse. Why am I still so often insensitive? I was spiritually arrogant." Again he fell silent, so I said, "That is the danger of the light; a little of it goes to the head, and makes one spiritually arrogant." "Yes," he answered, "but it was not for myself I was proud; it was for the light. In myself, I am only a little lens to catch a sunbeam and focus it." Smiling, I interrupted, "What is spiritual arrogance ever but pride of the lens in its office?" At once he answered, "And intellectual arrogance is pride of the knife in its blind dissecting."

Again we walked silently. Then he said, "Watching you in the cathedral, I saw in your face what I had recently laid bare in my own heart, the unacknowledged, the quite unconscious, hunger for salvation. And at once I knew that I must speak to you. To have kept silent would have been a betrayal of the very thing that had recently given me—blessedness."

The word jarred on me. I found myself saying inwardly, and how foolishly, "Oh God, please save me from being saved!" But immediately I was drawn toward the Christian, for he said, "Why, why can't I say these things without spoiling them, without making them sound pompous?"

He told me that by profession he was an engineer; that he had spent the years of the war far away in the East without his "dear wife"; that he had returned to find her a stranger, loving another, yet still dutiful to him, and anxiously willing to be at one with him again. So he set about to rewin her, and she to rediscover him. But it was useless. Rooted together, they had grown apart. Her torn tendrils, though reaching for him, bled for the other. So in the end, to free her, he had left her. For he loved her, so he told himself, far more than he craved her.

But when he had wrenched himself from her, his bared roots dried, his leaves withered.

He described himself as one of those lonely souls who, exiled from Europe, had maintained contact with the European spirit by reading. He mentioned Shakespeare, Dickens, Hardy, but few more modern. He claimed, however, also to be "well read in modern thought." He knew his Wells, his Shaw, his Freud, his Russell. Even Karl Marx he had read out there among the temples and the rice fields. These great writers, he said, had opened his eyes to the world. But now, this desolate homecoming was a new and a disintegrating experience. It fitted nowhere. Those modern prophets, he declared, could not help him; since for all their clever analysis they were spiritually imperceiving (so he phrased it). They could not see, and he himself till now had never seen, that if love fails life is worthless; and if love is not God (so he put it) all existence is pointless.

Formerly, though not unaware of evil, he had never looked squarely at it. There had been no need. Yet he had seen men beaten to death, and women mutilated, and he had responded with the required indignation. He knew also that savagery might conquer the whole planet. (Those lethal fungi that had sprouted once might sprout again.) All this he knew, but only as though from a book; or as a bad dream remembered in daytime. For him, evil had remained a thing unreal, in the end to be abolished from the planet. "I had two anchors," he said, "my love, and my faith in man's triumphant future. So long as these held, evil could only sadden, not shatter me."

But now, the anchor of his love had failed, and under the added strain, the other too had parted. "Evil at last," he said, "had its claws in my own heart. And through my own desolation I realized at last the evil of the universe."

He was silent. And I felt a frost creep in on me. For you and I, we too are held by that anchor. And if it should fail? Though our very differences enrich us, toughening our union, how can we know that some secret poison in one or the other cannot ruin us?

When the Christian had finished, I murmured vaguely of sympathy, but he sharply checked me. "Do not pity me," he said. "Rather envy; for it was only through suffering that my tight-shut eyes could be opened for salvation." In his voice I seemed to hear exaltation uneasily triumph over misery. "But God," he said, "had not yet scourged me enough. I was not yet ready to be saved."

He continued his story. He had a sister, a "beloved sister," and to her he had always turned in any distress. He praised her to me as "the soul of goodness." (Perhaps, like you, she was one of those who live most fully in giving life to others.) In his present misery he ran to her for comfort. But strangely, though she responded with the old young-motherly words of compassion, she remained withdrawn. The hand that she reached out to save him was now intangible, a mere phantom, always duly proffered, never to be grasped. Perplexed and sore, he drifted from her.

Presently this self-pitying brother learned that the sister was ill and in great suffering. Hurrying to her, he found that a secret pain had been too long ignored. And now, too late, the scalpel ferreted again and again through her body. The added torment was useless. Each time he visited her, the bars of her prison had moved in closer on that trapped, that ever outward-living and still life-hungry spirit. "How I dreaded," he said, "those eyes, that probed through mine for comfort!" For he, bitter from his life's failure and the new-felt evil of the universe, could give only phantom comforts, through which "those eyes" easily pierced to the inner desolation.

The frequent tides of her pain, he said, rose daily higher. They lapped her tethered body with corrosive waves, eating away little by little her humanity, till she was a mere wreck of whimpering nerves. His compassion tormented him, so that at last he implored the doctors to hasten her final sleep. But they refused, since the treatment, they affirmed, might still conquer. To the brother it seemed that they cared only for the interest of playing their losing game expertly to the end. This suspected ruthlessness was for him an added horror, a symbol of that coldly evil will which ruled (so he now believed) the whole universe.

All the while that the Christian had been telling me of these bitter experiences, we had been walking together in the sunny close. Small white clouds were

cherubs smiling down on us. Children were playing
on the grass. In a quiet corner a cat toyed with a half-
killed sparrow; until a girl rushed at it, and it fled
with its prey.

But now the Christian gripped my arm and halted
both of us. He said, "When my marriage broke, I felt
merely that all existence was pointless; but now, far
worse, I believed that the point, the meaning of it all,
was simply evil. Of course there was good, but only
to deepen the evil. There was love, to make cruelty
more subtle." Still holding my arm, he said with
bared teeth, "For consider! Think of all the evil of the
world! Two thousand million of us, and all of us
foully sick in a sick world." His hand fell from my
arm, and again we walked. He spoke of the great
host of bedridden sufferers, each in endless captivity;
and of those whose prison is penury; and the rest of
us, each with some unique private misery, unimaginable to any other. But mostly he dwelt on the
starkly evil will that secretly rules so many of us,
driving us constantly to hurt what is tender and
befoul what is fair. And God's will too now seemed to
him evil.

I felt that I ought to have been overwhelmed by all
this sum of horror that he had correctly enumerated.
But strangely I was divided between pity and aloofness. Out of the corner of my eye, I placidly, frivo-
lously, watched the life of the close: a youth with an
unlit cigarette considering whom he should ask for a
light; a mother trying to wipe the nose of an unruly
child; an old man on a seat enjoying the legs of the
passing girls.

The Christian said, "Coming away from my sister's death I walked the streets with nerves raw to all their horror. A dog crushed on the tarmac, an ignored beggar, a woman with a face of painted lead and eyes where (the harsh phrase jarred) "a festering soul was already stinking." These sights, he said, undermined his foundations. No future millennium could make such things never to have been. Eternity itself must stink with that soul's corruption. But he reminded himself that corruption was actually no worse and no better than saintliness.

One day, as the embittered engineer was passing the cathedral, he conceivd a resentful whim. He would insult the Power that masqueraded as Love. He strode in. The place was quiet. Sitting in the nave, he lounged and maintained a careful sneer, planning some bold free outrage. But the place was quiet and the few people ignored him. Presently he was absently studying the structure of column and vaulting; till defiance left him. Strange, he thought, how those old builders transformed efficient engineering with limited materials into high art! Soon he was marveling, as I had marveled, that stone should live and praise while in our hearts faith lies dead.

He considered those builders and their faith; and the long succession of robed ecclesiastics, vessels of an aged, a mellow and a potent wine. He considered the hosts of believers who had formerly thronged where now he sat alone; the ploughmen and housewives, the burghers and gentry. All were believers, however erring their conduct. All were participators in the communal delusion (as it then seemed to him) of love's divinity. In those past days, he supposed, the clouded minds of men were still warmly though vaguely irradiated by the already remote event that had blazed on the Cross. Sitting in that silent place, he tried, not out of reverence but through sheer curiosity and self-pitying resentment, to hear and if possible feel the far-off chanting of those worshippers. With quickened imagination he probed back still farther through the centuries to scrutinize objectively the reputed event itself. That individual, Jesus, if indeed he existed and was not merely a myth, must have been a man of singular sensitivity and intelligence; for he, before all others, clearly conceived (so we are told) that love is for all of us the way of life. And from this perception the remarkable Jew passed on to the conviction that love must be God. Living in an age before reason could expose the fallacy (for so it still seemed to this destined Christian), Christ easily persuaded himself that in the high experience of life he had indeed come face to face with God. And this exquisite delusion so kindled him that he was able to live his whole life as a shining, a dazzling example and symbol of love. And so, in the strength of his delusion, he became the star of a new faith.

So it seemed to this engineer, brooding in the bombed cathedral. But he reminded himself that the crucified prophet, in his last moments, had cried that his God had forsaken him. Those eyes, appealing to heaven, saw only the void.

Once more the Christian seized my arm and brought us face to face. He said, "But now, in that dark night of my despair, light began to dawn on me. I began to see that Christ alone gave meaning to this bleak, meaningless world."

He released my arm, and once more we paced the close. I noticed (but he paid no attention) that the sky was now all somber, and on the flagstones of our pathway a few large drops had fallen. Nursemaids were already encasing their struggling or patient charges in mackintoshes. A small boy, uncooperative, put out his tongue at heaven, in defiance or merely to catch raindrops.

Self-concerned, the Christian recounted the stages of his conversion. At last he was impelled to consider more and more earnestly the actual character of that remote and singular individual. But he could form no clear picture, so ignorant was he. He conceived only a passionately generous young man, intelligent, yet also in a way simple and even naive, preaching the life of love to a world incapable of it; till the world destroyed him. Yes, but that singular individual had indeed given men a vision of what they might be, if by miracle they could be raised a little beyond their brutishness. In his own person he had indeed shown them the life of love; shown them the divine spirit, the one thing worshipful.

I had been nodding approval. For how well we know, you and I, that in some deep way love is indeed divine; and that one and all we are vessels for that spirit.

But he went farther. Seizing my arm again, he said, "At this point the miracle happened. Without any aid from my intelligence or even my imagination, that unique person, Jesus, became an objective presence in my mind; and I saw that, though human, he was indeed God, the very God who is Love."

I moved impatiently, and the grip on my arm tightened. He continued speaking, and I listening. I began to feel that his conviction had hypnotic power. Once more, half in fantasy, half in earnestness, I prayed inwardly, "Oh God, save me from this salvation!" What was it that was happening to me?

"Do not," the Christian said, "tell me that this overwhelming vision of mine was the outcome in my mind merely of long-forgotten Christian teaching administered to me in childhood; or that it sprang from my own unconscious, figuring out for my guidance an ideal of life." He paused, searching my eyes; then continued, "I have myself considered that hypothesis, but it is not true to my actual experience. What could childhood, or my childish unconscious, give me like this shattering and remaking and entirely adult perception of the divine person?"

He released me, and again we walked. He did not notice that the rain was now tapping on our heads and shoulders, and rustling in the trees; so I steered him to shelter in the arched doorway. There we stood, between two small stone angels that prayed with joined hands and up-gazing eyes. From within, the chanting wanly sounded.

His talk had not ceased. It seemed to him, he said, that the actual life of that perfect human being unfolded before him in detail. With strange vividness, as though he had seen what he described, this transmuted engineer, this newborn Christian, told me how the actual life of Christ had confronted him. He believed (remember) or at least he thought he believed, that he had actually experienced the presence of the divine lover. No wonder his words had power; and even while I rebelled, I, too, almost believed that the man Jesus must indeed have been more than man.

The engineer said that he had watched all the phases of Christ's life. First the warm-hearted and resolute child, genial with playmates; but when they tormented a crippled sparrow, and would not listen to his pleading, he would furiously rout them. Then the boy on the Temple steps, confounding with sheer sincerity of feeling and fresh intelligence all the subtleties of the elders. The young man, gay companion and unfailing friend, who lived each moment fully yet without enslavement to it; for an inner voice constantly judged it, an inner light ruthlessly illuminated it; the voice and the light of his own waking divinity. Then the young man, already old in wisdom, freed of all self-concern, self-disciplined through and through to the spirit, scornfully rejecting Satan's lure of power, intent wholly on doing what God willed of him. Then the perfected man, discovering God within himself, waking fully to his own Godhead, and his self-chosen mission. Then his few years of lucid conduct and teaching, his friendliness for all outcast persons, his fierce challenge to all heartlessness. And then his death, agonized less by bodily pain than by pity for man's blind self-wounding harshness.

While the Christian was watching Christ's life unfold (like an opening flower, he said) the adult spirit of that perfect man was constantly and overwhelmingly present to him; inwardly yet objectively, as the beloved may be present to the lover in absence.

The Christian's account of his master's life had deeply moved me. Looking back, I cannot understand why I should have been so stirred; but it did at the time seem to me that a lovely and overmastering presence confronted me through the window of the Christian's words. While an inner voice quietly warned me, another voice called me. I felt myself tottering on the brink of the Christian salvation. Yet I knew quite clearly that if I took that plunge I should be damned; and worse, I should have been false to the light.

As the Christian spoke, I had been absently looking at the features of the stone angel beside me. A forgotten artist had carved them with restraint and power. Whether Christ were God or not God, the spirit that Christ preached was excellently signified in the stone. Presently a little spider strayed across the statue's brow, traversed its eye, wandered down its nose, and from the tip launched itself into space, swaying and gyrating on its thread. It landed at last on the joined hands. Strangely this outrage did not sully the angel's glory; heightened it rather, stressing that this fair messenger was not, after all an actual, a living yet supernatural being, but inanimate stone and a symbol. A symbol of the spirit. Well, and Jesus? Surely his true glory also was not that he was a supernatural being, descended out of heaven, but that he was a human individual (actual or fictitious) whose life, through its unique perfection, had become a symbol reigning in the hearts of men, and strengthening them with the vision of love's divinity.

While I was musing about Christ as symbol, the Christian, with downcast eyes, was telling me how, in the light of that bright presence, and of the virtue of the God-man's conduct here on earth, he came to realize with increasing shame and horror the true condition of his own soul, and the ugliness of his own conduct. "My sister," he said, "whom I thought I loved so deeply, I never loved at all. Indeed, how could I love her, never having really known her, save as a comfort for myself? And when at last she failed me, I was resentful. My wife, too, I never loved. Even when I surrendered her, loving her (so I told myself) more than I craved her, the truth was simply that, with her heart elsewhere, she was useless to me; and so, striking a generous pose, I left her. It was the same with all my self-righteous indignation at the barbarities of war. This too was a mere gesture, its nerve not love but a vulgar tangle of mere squeamishness and pride."

With a rueful smile he looked at me and said, "Pathetic! That we should so deceive ourselves!"

Continuing his story, he reminded me that he had entered the cathedral to commit some outrage; but now, he said, he had sat for a long time paralyzed with self-loathing because of his new perception of the spirit which his whole life had violated.

Presently (he said) he found himself kneeling with his face bowed in his hands and tears breaking from his closed eyes. His lips formed the silent words, "Oh God, unmake me, destroy me! I have ruined the soul that you created."

At last, he said, the miracle was completed. Christ took full possession of him. His old self-absorbed self fainted into nothingness (or so he believed) and in its place awoke a new self, wholly directed to God. He knew, of course, that he would sin a thousand times daily, through inveterate frailty; but he knew that he was saved.

Yet in a way, he said, he cared little that he was a saved soul, for he was wholly intent upon the loveliness of the spirit that possessed him. He had in a manner outgrown even the desire for salvation. "Strange," he said, "that, although the unregenerate self violently craves immortality, yet when it is killed and reborn, and assured of fulfillment in eternity, it counts this a negligible fact. Its whole beatitude is that now, without any thought of self, it sees God and adores him, and wills only to perform God's will of it." I quicky interposed, "Then why, if you no longer craved eternal life, must you still believe that we do in fact live on eternally as individuals?" He paused, smiling. "That was a shrewd question," he said. There was silence before he answered, "I can say only that I *see* our immortality, I *see* our eternal reality. Also, if God should neglect to save his creatures, he would be less than the divine lover, and so not worshipful."

Ignoring my wry face, he pursued his story of his conversion in the cathedral. For a while he had continued kneeling in inarticulate worship, but presently he allowed his gaze and his thoughts to range happily over the cool stonework and the listless, vaguely groping sightseers. It became clear to him that, since Christ had saved him, he must in gratitude fit himself to be a servant of Christ. He must equip himself to the utmost of his power with the traditional wisdom of Christ's Church. So he diffidently approached a priest and begged for guidance. For many weeks he read the scriptures and the records of the saints; and every day he came into the cathedral to pray alone or to take part in the services.

"And now," he said, "I began to discover meaning in all the well-worn doctrines of the Church that formerly had seemed so silly or incredible. For instance, the doctrine of the Trinity began to be intelligible to me. How clear it is that, while God must be thought of as indivisibly one, he must also be three-fold! He must, of course, be the omnipotent Creator; but also he must be the divine Lover, distinct from omnipotence so as to suffer the whole depth of pain and misery; but also he must be the Holy Spirit, emanating from the Creator, inspiring the Lover, and beckoning all of us."

Triumphantly the Christian's eyes sought mine, demanding assent. When my brows puckered, he smiled, as though to a dull child whom one must not discourage. Then, reverting to a simpler matter, more suited to my halting intelligence, he said, "And think again of immortality! When at last my heart was opened to receive the full light and warmth of Christ's divinity, it became clear to me that, though indeed the evil in us must be utterly destroyed, the essential and particular spirit that each of us is *must* be secured of eternal life through Christ's love. I saw that my sister, generous soul, *must* (since God is love) find bliss in eternity, and with her, all of us *must* be destined for salvation; save perhaps some few who irrevocably damn themselves through impenetrable hardness of heart. But for my part I have faith that even these are won by the Love that is all-powerful."

"But how can you know," I protested, "how can you possibly know that Love is God, is an almighty being who rules the universe?" He replied fervently, "I tell you, my heart *sees* unmistakably that it is so."

Searching my unlit face, he added, "You also shall
see. Through me, Christ will save you." We both fell
silent. Then he continued his gentle attack on my
unbelief. "My friend," he said, "you yourself have
already seen that without Christ the universe is
unintelligble and unendurably horrible. You are
now beginning to see that through Christ a meaning
springs to the eye. All the evil of the world, which so
dismayed you when I first saw you, turns out to be
for our own good, to chasten us, to waken us to the
spirit; that we may all at last blissfully live the life of
the spirit in eternity." Again he watched me in silent
expectation.

I did not answer. Avoiding his gaze, I looked across
the close. The rain was now hissing on the flagstones, each drop a bullet with splashing impact. A
yellow butterfly, shot down by the first volley, feebly
struggled on the wet ground, its wings muddy. From
within, since the short service was over, the worshippers were issuing one by one; a few dim women, an
elderly man, and also, rather self-consciously, a soldier. Each glanced upward, frowning at the deluge.
Some put up umbrellas and hurried away; some
waited in the porch to shelter. Newcomers to the
cathedral stamped their feet and shook the water
from their clothing.

I did not answer, because I was desperately perplexed. How intelligible, how humane and friendly,
the Christian's account of the ancient faith now
seemed to me! I thought of you. How humanly right
it seemed that you should be yourself in eternity;
purged, no doubt, transfigured; but essentially and

recognizably yourself, the unique particular being whose life I share! And how right that I, purged almost beyond recognition, should be with you eternally! The annihilation of our union did indeed seem to make nonsense of the universe.

Yes, and this loving, this spirit that holds us together and raises each of us to a higher level of awareness in relation to the whole universe—could I deny, had I any need to deny, that in *some* sense it was divine? This spirit, that so quickened us, must surely be the quickening spirit of the whole universe, and the only way of universal fulfillment. And had I not at least seen that this spirit of love, if it is indeed divine, *must* in some way be personified in a supreme undividual, who out of charity needs must bear all the sins of the world, needs must suffer in his own heart all the evil of all the worlds? And had I not, under this Christian's influence, felt at last that Jesus was in fact this perfect embodiment of the divine love?

And so, and so . . . But on the very brink of the abyss, vertigo seized me, and a will to surrender to the gulf of this salvation.

The little spider had by now climbed back along his rope and had strung another from the statue's nose to its chin, and from chin to breast, laboriously constructing the framework for its web. The Christian, following the direction of my gaze, saw the silken threads and their minute author. With a careless hand he swept the threads from the statue's face and blew the spider from his fingers.

Suddenly I knew that to demand eternal life for the individual, even for the beloved, even for you, was childish, and a betrayal. Love was indeed the way of life; and maybe in so dark a sense, which is at present inconceivable, it presides in the very heart of the universe; but to pledge oneself to this belief would nevertheless be for me a grave betrayal of spiritual integrity. Calmly, and without dismay, even with unreasoning joy, I reminded myself that you and I, loved and loving, might well in fact be short-lived sparkles, merely, in an age-old pyrotechnic. The vastness of the physical confronted me, the boundless void and the astronomical aeons; before man; before the planets congealed; before the oldest of the stars first spangled the nebulae; before the unnumbered host of the nebulae themselves condensed from the expanding cloud of the young cosmos; back to the initial and inscrutable creative act, the atom bomb from which all sprang.

Hugeness is in itself nothing, but it has significance. For if this little world of ours, this grain, can in its lowly way harbor the spirit, what of the whole? The hugeness of space and time did not dismay me. I accepted it with grave joy, awed less by its threat than by pregnancy.

And so, our little loving is indeed hesitantly significant; if not of the inscrutable heart of all things, at least of the splendor that the cosmos may support in countless worlds, happy and tragic.

And now I saw once more quite clearly that what matters, what finally claims allegience is not the individual nor even mankind, but something else, which all of us together, on earth and in all worlds, imperfectly manifest. This something, I told myself, this spirit, is indeed the music of the spheres, for which we are all lowly instruments and players. Whether this music is only to be appreciated gropingly by the players themselves, or whether it is for the discerning joy of some cosmical artist, or perhaps in some incomprehensible way for the very music itself, we cannot know. Perhaps it is for nothing. On that high plane thought is impotent.

Then you and I? If the end is sleep, all's well. For we have lived. Or if in death we do indeed wake into some ampler life, to contribute further to the music, then again all's well. If we live on, it is for the music; if we die, equally it is for the music.

The rain had stopped. The trees heavily dripped. Sunshine drew from the moist ground vapors and fragrances. The drowned butterfly lay still. Presently the cat, emerging from some shelter, strode haughtily, with the mouse limp between its teeth.

But now the Christian, who had so patiently waited, was saying, "At last you are seeing (are you not?) that Christ redeems all suffering." I could not answer, except by a gesture of perplexity.

While I was searching for a reply, a starling alighted by the dead butterfly, cocked an eye in our direction, gobbled the prize, stood for a moment quizzically regarding me with its head on one side, squawked insolently and then took wing.

Suddenly I saw the Christian and myself as two large and solemn bipeds making strange noises at each other. The words that I had been using in my own mind echoed in my memory as poor animal calls laboring to signify things utterly beyond their range. How can the primitive grunts of any terrestrial animal ever signify truth about the depths and heights of reality? The little net of human discourse can sample only the ocean's surface, and all its harvest is flotsam. How should it possibly reach down to the beauties and horrors of the deep? Human reason, a fluttering moth, can never soar.

Then what, I asked myself, was the appropriate attitude to the dark-bright, hideous-lovely Whole? Fear? Proud rebellion? Obsequious worship? Rather, I told myself, a difficult blend of acceptance in the heart and cold scrutiny in the mind.

Acceptance, merely? For a moment the presence of the Whole, or of some greater thing beyond the Whole, seemed to bear down upon me in inconceivable majesty. My heart whispered, "Thou! Oh, Thou!"

But immediately another thought, another prayer, was wrung from me. "Oh, let my heart strongly feel that presence, but let my mind be utterly silent before it. For even if I say, 'Thou! Oh, Thou,' I say too much."

Praying in this strange way, I laughed.

Thereupon the Christian, mistaking my long silence and final bark of laughter, slipped his arm in mine and said, "My friend you have won through. Merciful Christ has saved you."

But at his touch I had stiffened, and now his arm retreated. Our eyes met, and for a long moment each searched the other.

I was preparing to do battle against his proselytizing, and to conquer his faith. But his eyes checked me. For his Christ had indeed saved him from his self-loving despair; and without his Christ he might be lost. In his present state of partial waking (so I told myself, perhaps complacently) he could not endure the severer vision.

So I said, "You have been very good to me, and very patient. But the upshot is that your way is not mine. You need belief; for me it is unnecessary. Without it I travel lighter, yes and perhaps farther. Strangely, in my unbelief I gain full peace, the peace that passes understanding. And joy too. I have found joy in the sheer given reality, with all its dark-bright beauty. Light has come to you in one way, to me in another. And though you have not won me, I am grateful to you. Let neither of us grudge the other his vision."

He was silent for some time. Then in a low voice he said, "I think you do not fully know what suffering is, and the illumination that it brings. May God take all joy from you, may he torment you as he tormented me, so that at last your eyes may be opened, and the true light may save you."

Smiling, I offered my hand in parting. He gripped it, and we stood in silence. Then, he said, "God works in a mysterious way. If ever you need me I will help you." And I, laughing, replied, "And if someday your faith fails you, remember there is another way, and perhaps I can help." I left him.

Looking back, I saw him standing between the two stone angels, his eyes downcast, under the grooved archway, under the great west front that bombs had marred.

Well, I have told you. And in your presence my mind runs clearer. For now I see that, though on a certain level the truth was mainly on my side, it was marred by an unwitting complacency, an intellectual and perhaps a spiritual arrogance. I did not after all take deeply enough to heart my own mind's inadequacy. Perhaps a more awakened consciousness would have seen in that Christian's faith a deeper truth than in my skepticism. Was he after all right when he said that I needed more of suffering?

Perhaps! But even so, must I not at all costs be true to my own light, never pretending to reach farther than its beam can search? Yes, and I *gladly* choose the clear cold brightness of my vision, though darkness surrounds it. I prefer it to the Christian's more comfortable glow and warmth. I am loyal to it because it reveals more to me and demands more of me.

A Scientist

I have met a scientist, and now I must tell you about him.

It was at the party, the congested, the conglomerate party, where I was taken "to meet people." If you had been with me, perhaps I could have made contact, but the man who had brought me was too soon swept from me by the throng's glacier drift. The few whom he had burdened with me had tried to include me, but we could find no catalytic. I was a goat penned among sheep. The bleating was alien to me, though alas not meaningless. With each new guest's arrival, the flood of sound rose higher. I was a trapped miner, the water rising toward his mouth.

Yet many of these people were individually notable. From press photographs I recognized a cabinet minister, two famous writers, a popular actress, an eminent scientist. Among the bright female silks and the male motley of black and white, there was a high ecclesiastic in purple tunic and breeches. His face was old sandstone, crowned with snow; and under the white cornices of his brows gleamed serpent eyes, of wisdom or of cunning. Individually distinguished, and leaders of my species in this island, why should these creatures seem to me in my loneliness a bunch of chattering monkeys?

Across the room, a young man stood alone in silence. His glass was empty. His cigarette ash dropped unnoticed. Intently, and with a secret smile, he reviewed the huddled flock. I thought of a sparrow hawk on a high branch, watching for prey; then of a mongrel terrier, scruffy, genial, mischievous, none too clean, with mud unnoticed on his muzzle. He was a raw-boned young man, wire-haired, with terrier eyes, and a complexion of uncooked shrimps.

I struck boldly into a current that was setting in his direction. When I had emerged beside him, I waited a little, for decency, and to recover composure; then I said casually, "Do you know these people, mostly? I am told they are all distinguished, all leaders of our society." His response was delayed. Judicially, he replied, "Five percent, perhaps, I know; maybe seven. Leaders? Yes, of stampeding swine, heading for the precipice." There was silence. "These occasions," I ventured, "terrify me. Silly, isn't it!" He answered at once, "Just boring, I call them. When I find myself stranded, I play a game. I study the fauna." Silence fell once more, so I reminded him of my presence by remarking that a crowd of strangers did often strike one as mere fauna.

To my surprise he let loose a flood of fantasy, couched in a jargon that was consciously literary. "First," he said, "I observe that these creatures are all specimens of *Homo sapiens,* and at bottom paleolithic savages, though tricked out modernistically in tissues of vegetable fiber or animal hair, or the secretion of caterpillars, with here and there scraps of hide, bits of metal, and a sprinkling of rare crystals. That priest in fancy dress is the successful medicine man, skilled in spells, the practiced ventriloquist who makes the great idol speak laws or threats. That major there, unbelievably kilted, I see as a tribal warrior, with naked cart-horse muscles and a girdle of scalps. That other's waistcoated paunch might never have reached such magnitude in the hard early days of the species; but reduce it somewhat, and you have the bulging and sweaty headman of the tribe, already past his rule, soon to be done away with by the scalp-girdled one. In the corner, there, a born herd leader wallows in the admiration of those withered women and those youths. See how his ears are pricked for every tremor of opinion, how he laps up the public's whims, to regurgitate them later as his own God-given gospel."

I laughed, and was at ease, sharing the superiority of this little hawk on its high perch; or watching this queerly sophisticated terrier sniffing out vermin.

He continued. "Next I undress them, and see them all nakedly huddled together. And of course naked they really are. That woman with the creased face and bloody claws—I take off her fashioned dress and corsets to observe the sagging belly, the flapping dugs like empty hot-water bottles. The paunched headman, stripped of all trappings, becomes a sheer grizzled human gorilla. That young bitch of the species, all sexed up for market, is now unpainted, unpermed, disheveled, grimy with soot and grease and blood from her savage cooking. And how she stinks! Yet to the prime young male, there, the slut is

a seductive morsel. See how he leans toward her! His nakedness betrays an excitement which clothes conveniently mask."

I was enjoying his fantasy. It appealed strongly to the terrier in myself. But a vague protest was brewing in me. I thought of you, so real in person; beneath your simplicity, so complex; in all your doing, so well orientated to the spirit. Did this young man, I wondered, suppose that by stripping the human onion of its coats he would expose some indestructible core of brute humanity?

He continued. "The next gambit goes deeper. Take away from each of them all that is human. But preserve for identification some characteristic feature of each individual; for instance, that paunch, and that priestly dignity, and that lusty musculature. Let us operate on the asking bitch there. We must recreate the ape in her, or at least the subhuman, while somehow preserving the demurely lascivious expression of her whole face. First, then, thicken her, bandy her legs, tip her forward with knuckles to earth for support. Cover her breasts and her whole body with coconut hair. Cut away her saucy chin and her lips like fruit, and plaster them above her eyes to harden into a great brow ridge. Snip off her nose, revealing the septum. Forget there's meaning in her chatter (if there is), and hear it as sheer auditory sex stimulation, almost as heady to the male as her sexual stink."

He flashed a gleeful look at me; as though the terrier, in his enthralling investigation, had spared a moment to look round and say, "Good fun, isn't it!"

He said, "When you have had enough of her in this

near-human repulsiveness, you can amuse yourself by shrinking her to a little goggle-eyed wire-fingered tarsier, scampering along branches and twigs. Then, if you like, see her (always with her expression of veiled bawdiness) as the primitive, undifferentiated mammal. Or remake her still more radically to be a monotreme. Now the young male will have to be content with a cruder and less intimate sexual contact, since he must copulate without penetration. And she will lay eggs. It is a delicate but an amusing operation to remold that marble and sculptured human arm of hers stage by stage back to the sketchy forelimb of a lizard, altering the set of the bones, the proportions of each muscle. And for those Atalanta legs of hers (which one easily pictures under the silk dress) we must achieve a still more radical feat of plastic surgery, crooking them, splaying them sideways, reducing the plump buttocks almost to extinction, and parting them to make room for a great crocodile tail. Now watch her go slithering among (or over) her fellow reptiles, while the male, chained by the nose to the bawdy smell of her, slobbers along behind."

He paused, and I sniggered politely, but anxiously. Again he shot his terrier glance at me and said, "You think I am unfair to her; but after all, that is what she really is even now, under the knickers and the brassiere, in spite of the breasts and the vagina, and the human hypertrophy of the cerebral cortex."

All I could say was, "But if you take away so much of her, where is she?" He answered, "She, of course, is what we see before us *and* what I have laid bare; but what I have laid bare is the controlling mechanism of the whole system even now." "But, but—" I said, and fell silent.

He resumed his fantasy. "The game can be continued indefinitely. When one is in the mood one can reduce the creatures to the amphibian, the fish, the worm, the microorganism. Or one may vary it by retaining their human shapes but seeing them inwardly as physiological going concerns. Under the skin see the blood-soaked muscles, pumping blood or air or words; or composing themselves to idiotic smiles or affected laughter; or churning food. The bitch, for instance, has a stomach, a muscular bag stuffed now with sandwiches and cocktails, which it assiduously mixes, till the pulp is ripe for passing down through the tangle of tubing that her neat belly conceals. Meanwhile that crumpled muscular hosepipe, seething like a nest of snakes, is probably dealing with a half-digested mess of chops and chips. And further still, the unwanted rubbish is collecting, to be ejected in due course into the socially approved recepticle. The creature also has a brain, a fantastically subtle texture of fibers, which even now are being activated in inconceivably complex and coordinate rhythms. Mentally these neural events have the form of (presumably) a perception of the young male as an eligible mate, and a using of every wile (primitive and sophisticated) to catch him. Meanwhile at the other end of her anatomy, stored in a recess convenient for access by the male seed, her egg is ripe. It is a pinhead; but it is a continent still mainly unexplored by science. Somewhere within its vast yet microscopic interior lie, meticulously located, all the factors for reproduction of her kind, and indeed of her own special idiosyncrasies, even down to that intriguing twist of the left eyebrow. And if ever she is so careless as to have a child, its whole physique and temperament will be an expression of the chancy collocation of genes (her's and her mate's) in the union of sperm and ovum; in conjunction, of course, with the appropriate environment."

"You are very sure," I said. He replied, "There is no certainty, but the probability is overwhelming."

Then he started a new gambit, saying, "Now let us expose the bitch's fundamental structure. It is an inconceivably complex tissue of the ultimate physical particles or wavetrains, say 10^{12n} of protons, electrons, positrons, neutrons and perhaps other units still to be discovered. Thus the bitch keeps her Atalanta figure, her human complexion, her fruity lips; but within their volume, within the contours of breast, buttock and so on, one must conceive a great void, fretted by midges of electromagnetic potency." The young man paused, then concluded, "But in the end the game palls. It is the early moves that stimulate."

His flight of fantasy seemed to have spent itself. Presently I asked him, "Are you a writer? You have a quick imagination, and you seem to care about words." For his ornate and rather stilted speech had puzzled me. "God, no!" he said. "I am a geneticist, but addicted to verbiage off duty." Then with a sidelong look to measure me he added, "A geneticist, you know, is a biologist who studies inheritance." I replied politely that his profession must be indeed interesting, an endlessly enthralling adventure. He laughed deprecatingly, and said, "Counting flies with black tummies or misshapen wings, breeding monstrosities from nature's well-tried normalities is humdrum work." "But," I said, "the significance of it all!" With a sigh he answered, "The minutiae are so exacting that one almost loses sight of the significance. But doubtless we shall someday produce human monstrosities, men with tails or two heads, or tricks like the waltzing mouse, or special lusts for obedience, or coal mining, or cleaning lavatories."

Provokingly I added, "Or perhaps for the life of the spirit?" The words clearly jarred on his scientific mind, like obscenity in a church, or prayer in a laboratory. After a silence he said, "I have no use for words that are mere emotive noises without clear significance."

We both fell dumb. Presently I ventured, "Tell me! What is your real aim in genetic research?" Without hesitation he answered, "To earn a living; and by work that is not too irksome. Incidentally, of course, impulses of curiosity, self-assertion, cooperation and so on find a healthy outlet." I waited for more, then prompted him, "Is that all? Is there no sense of a calling, or participation in a great common enterprise?" After a further silence he said, "No! That is really all. But greater definition is possible. The study of inheritance appears to be socially desirable, for the advancement of our species. And I, as a social animal and humanly intelligent, direct my social impulses to that end—so far as this can be done without frustrating my far stronger self-regard."

The slow swirl of the crowd had swept us into an

alcove, and there, cast high and dry on a window seat, we were almost in seclusion.

I questioned, "What precisely do you mean by 'the advancement' of the species?" He lightly replied, "Oh, more pleasure and less pain for its members; and for this end more power over its environment and over human nature itself. That is where we geneticists come in. We seek control of other species for man's sake, and ultimately the manipulation of man's own genetic makeup, so as to abolish disease and all other grave frustrations, and to evoke new possibilities of pleasurable activity." I asked if he would maintain that up to our day science had in fact increased the possibility of pleasure. "Surely!" he answered. "What with the radio, the cinema, improved travel and so on." I added to his list improved warfare, industrial servitude, modern engines of oppression and mass production of stereotyped minds. But he protested that all this was the consequence not of science itself but of man's foolish use of science. "Man's purposes," he said, "are in the main still primitive. Little by little science itself will change them. For science will become man's wise ruler instead of his misused slave. At present the affairs of the species are directed by scientifically uneducated politicians, charlatans whose policy is determined merely by the need to pander either to the money magnates or to the ignorant swarms in the trade unions."

I commented, "So you would have the scientists themselves rule society." He answered, "Social affairs should of course be directed by the relevant experts in each field." "And who," I demanded, "is to control the experts?" "Why, of course," he said, "the scientifically educated public. And scientists will have to see to it that the whole really educable population is educated scientifically. Surely that is the reasonable goal. Meanwhile, we must pin our faith to the gradual spread of the scientific spirit."

I challenged him, "Are you really confident that science has increased men's pleasure and reduced their pain? Are you quite sure that the mediaeval peasant's life was less pleasurable and more distressful than the modern industrial worker's?" With an affectation of patience, he replied, "All that we actually know is that the wretches were undernourished, undersized, crippled by disease, harddriven by the landlords and the priests, tormented by religious superstition. Perhaps they enjoyed their condition, but it seems unlikely." "On the other hand," I suggested, "their environment was perhaps more appropriate to their biological nature than the industrial environment. They seem to have enjoyed the round of the seasons and all the varied processes of tillage. And they were securely anchored to the conviction that—well, that goodness mattered." "Goodness," he retorted, with some exasperation, "is another of those emotive noises that mean nothing. And surely it is well known that today primitive peasants all over the world (and they must be very like the mediaeval sort) are only too eager to give up their primitive ways and enjoy the amenities that science offers." I answered, "Oh yes! The poor creatures are given alcohol and the cinema, and soon they crave these drugs, and succumb to them."

Evidently my companion felt that he had proved

his case, for he ignored my reply, and said, "But to return to the motives of the geneticist. He is mainly kept going by sheer lust of discovery. Intelligence, you see, clamors for exercise, even if only in crossword puzzles. But there is another motive. We crave power; and, being highly social, we crave it not merely in competition with others but also in the cooperative service of our species. At the back of all our minds, I suspect, is this sublimation of the crude lust of power." I provoked him by enquiring if the will to serve the species could be satisfied merely by providing it with more gadgets, amenities, titillations. He shot a wary glance at me before replying, "In the last resort, I suppose, what we want to give our species is not *just* pleasure, just any sort of pleasure, but the pleasure of power, the satisfaction of the cunning and resolute animal conquering its environment. Evolution favors in the long run the more developed types, those that show more versatility and adaptability in securing power over the environment. Yes! We want to give man greater power over his environment. We want him to be master of his world, and perhaps of other worlds; and of his own nature and destiny."

"But tell me!" I insisted. "What is he to *do* with his power? *What* destiny should be choose?"

The young man shrugged. "That," he said, "is not really my affair. Presumably he should choose to make the most of himself and his world, to impress himself as vigorously as possible on the universe. You see, between organism and environment there is constant action and reaction. Through the pressure of man's actual environment the universe makes man what in fact he is; and since, through automatic natural selection, it has made him sensitive, intelligent and versatile, he reacts strongly and effectively on the universe. What in the last resort he should choose depends, I suppose, on what his nature finally demands for fullest satisfaction, what in the last resort he *pleases* to do." I said, "For you, then, the final criterion is always the feeling of pleasure. The question, what *ought* man to please to do, is meaningless. Have I understood you?" He paused before replying, and again he shot a wary glance at me. Then cautiously he said, "In a sense the individual 'ought' to serve the species; for only in the advancement of the species can he find the deepest satisfaction." I asked, "But if he does not, as a matter of fact, *want* to serve the species, if he wants merely individual advantage and personal luxury, does the 'ought' not apply to him at all?" "In the final analysis," he answered, "it does not. The statement that he 'ought' to do otherwise merely registers the fact that he is blind to the greatest satisfaction, enthralled to lesser pleasures, which if he were wise and resolute, he would sacrifice. Apart from this, 'ought' is meaningless, an outgrown relic of our subjection to parental authority and the convention of the herd."

A little wearily, a little sadly and without facing me; a little in the style of the senior amiably condescending to the junior (though I was twice his age), he gave me a cigarette. The terrier had for the time vanished, and in its place I saw a bored old hound. We smoked in silence, watching the throng.

Presently I said to my companion, "You scientists, and above all you biologists, seem very sure that in the end you will be able to analyze out the whole of human nature, leaving no unexplained residue." He

replied, "Our confidence is strengthened every day.
Anyone who spends his life on detailed, and on the
whole impressively successful, analysis is bound to
realize that the main mechanisms of human behavior are by now as well established as the principles of
engineering. Genes, Mendelian laws, the central
nervous system, hormones, individual and social
conditioning leave no excuse for postulating a surd.
Of course much remains to be discovered, but by now
it is quite clear that our nature is strictly determinate, and systematic through and through."

"To the cobblers," I said, "there's nothing like
leather! How can you be so confident that science
cannot mislead us. It does, of course, throw a bright
beam in some directions; but does it, perhaps, impose
a deeper darkness in others? May not the very fact of
your absorption in the minutiae of your special skill
have blinded you to other kinds of experience?"

The party was now disintegrating, and my companion rose to leave. He said, "It is of course possible.
But science is a varied and a well-criticized discipline. And the beam searches in *every* direction.
Success has been spectacular. It is difficult to doubt
that the course of progressive thought will henceforth be set by science."

As we were parting, I asked him to spare time for a
dinner and another talk. Nonchalantly he accepted,
and we fixed a date. As as afterthought he invited
me to "look in at the Department first," and he would
perhaps be able to show me some impressive things.

In due course I appeared at his Department. He
took me into a room lined with shelves that were

loaded with bottles. In the center and also under the window were tables bearing many rectangular glass tanks, each containing in miniature the appropriate environment of some beast under study, and in each of these artificial worldlets the creatures listlessly lived.

My companion called out a girl's name, and from another room came an undecorated but not ignorable young woman in trousers and a little threadbare jacket that coped gallantly with her ample breasts. With a man-to-man downrightness she gripped my hand, smiling firmly. But her lips in repose were luscious, and her eyes, though superficially sparkling, were deep as the Atlantic or the evening zenith. Her hair, glossy as old well-polished leather, was drawn severely back; but it too was of a generous nature, revolting against discipline. A heavy strand drooped over one ear, needing constant attention. A hairpin projected from the large but disintegrating bun on her nape. I confess her presence distracted me somewhat from the lowlier fauna.

The two young human specimens, prattling in their biologist's jargon (sprinkled with modern slang) displayed their living treasures. Now and then they spoke of the great man who was their chief and their teacher. They spoke with most irreverent ridicule of his leaning toward religion and his faith in liberalism; but behind their words lurked awe and affection.

Toward each other, these two behaved always with the familiarity and swift understanding that comes to well-tried workmates; but also with a flow of genial banter that was evidently in some way necessary to them to preserve their independence from each other, and to smooth the flow of their common life, their queer symbiosis. For it was evident that in some way each depended on the other, and at the same time was defensive against the other. I soon noticed, too, a subtle difference in their behavior. While he negligently, almost unwittingly (or was he all the while consciously acting?), performed the ritual of comradeship, she responded with a friendliness that was deliberate and attentive. But I suspected an undercurrent of soreness.

Toward all their creatures, their foster children, they both behaved as though scientific detachment were awkwardly complicated by a sort of shamefaced parental fondness. I was indeed enthralled by their creatures; yet my attention often strayed to themselves, isolated for so much of their time here in this tank, this test tube; as though some superhuman experimenter had singled them out for study, hoping to gain through observation of their mutual reactions new understanding of the human species.

They showed me newts, lizards, frogs; and also (even more distant cousins of Queen Victoria and Jesus Christ) innumerable flies imprisoned in bottles. Some of these creatures were normal products of evolution; some were precious monstrosities, evoked by human ingenuity, and kept alive by a more than maternal devotion. Ordinary newts, with their bladelike tails and inadequate legs (as though copied from a small child's drawing), hung suspended in the water, or glided through the subaqueous jungle, or clambered into the air. But a few were patently and shockingly not ordinary. One such creature miserably supported the burden of two heads. Another carried a half-formed twin attached to his back. Turning from these oddities, I was shown a normal crested newt (called Archibald). He was induced to display his flamelike ornament by the infuriating sight of his own reflection in a bit of mirror. An axolotl, a pallid and feebly animated sausage, inadequately quadruped, stared vacuously, unconscious of his significance for science. Little black lizards, mercurial in the girl's warm hand, were slender as snakes. A unique snake displayed vestigial limbs. Toads lumbered over stones and herbage, bestirring themselves for the chopped meat that was dropped for them. Swarms of little crustaceans, mere fidgeting points of life, explored their bit of ocean or pond for food. Snails clung to leaves or stones. It was pointed out to me that the spiral of the shell was generally coiled clockwise, but occasionally in the opposite direction. And this oddity, I was told, was of special interest because its inheritance depended on the mother alone. The bodies of these creatures, it seems, are asymmetrical through and through, and the dextral and sinistral individuals are mirror images of each other. The young biologist delighted to explain that, since the genital organ is on one side of the head alone, dextrals and sinistrals could never mate with each other, but only with their own kind.

Throughout this scientific exposition, the two humans maintained their banter, snowballing each other with argument, evidence and technical terms.

I heard much of allelomorphs, of dominants and recessives, of haploid, of polymorphic varieties, of the exact location of genes on chromosomes.

Leaving the tanks, the young man selected from a certain shelf a certain bottle. There were scores, hundreds, of such bottles, each housing a population of flies; and each population was the issue of some planned interbreeding. A whiff of ether reduced the selected population to temporary impotence, so that they could be poured out on a microscope slide for observation. As I peered through the instrument, the couple spoke of the minute significant differences that I should see, the ruddier and the yellower eyes, the hairy or bald bodies, the stumpy or long antennae, the serviceable or crippled wings. "We have now," the young man said, "recorded nearly a million mutations." His companion took up the thread. "Mostly they are lethal, or at best indifferent; but with them we have mapped out on the chromosomes practically the whole inheritance mechanism of this species." He displayed a printed volume wherein all this work was recorded. "Someday," he said, "our ancestors will have an equally full account of inheritance in man, covering his physical and his mental characters, down to the least idiosyncrasy. The job will, of course, be far more complicated; but there is little doubt that we shall in time analyze out the whole mechanism of human inheritance, and so the basic structure of human nature." The girl continued the theme. "In the end," she said, "we shall breed men as we breed horses and dogs and cattle, creating different types for different functions within the world society; lovers of the tropics and of the arctic, of mining and of flying, of leadership and of obedience, of creative action and of routine, of interplanetary exploration and of terrestrial homekeeping." The young man smiled at me, and winked. He said, "She is rather uncritically sublimating her maternal instinct. Unconsciously, she would like to mother the whole lot." The girl laughed, and replied spiritedly, "Muddleheaded amateur psychologist!"

The show was now over, and the couple were preparing to leave the Department. Taking his mackintosh from behind a door, the young geneticist said, "Well, now you have seen a little of our world, perhaps you can understand why we are confident in science." I concluded my little speech of thanks rather tactlessly, by remarking that science had been said to give power without wisdom. He swung round and faced me to say, "Don't you see that wisdom *follows* from power. The helpless savage has no wisdom. Wisdom arises only in civilization, and civilization is an expression of economic production." Taking a final glance round the room, he opened the door, adding, "Of course there's a time lag. And so long as our affairs are controlled by ignorant politicians there's a real danger that the wisdom inherent in man's new powers will be frustrated, and the species will destroy itself. Atomic power is a dangerous toy."

I said we must pursue the matter over dinner; and I invited the girl to accompany us. She glanced quickly at her colleague, then refused, excusing herself on the plea that she had work to do at home.

And so, after thanks and adieus, I took the young man alone to a restaurant.

My new friend sipped his sherry with serious attention, savoring, analyzing, registering the complex experience. Perhaps he noticed that I was amused by his earnestness, for presently he said, "It is wonderful how even the minor experiences repay observation." "Yes," I answered, "but if one attends too closely to some particular field of the universe one has no attention for others." Sighing, he replied, "True indeed! I shall never be an expert wine taster." "The great thing," I suggested, "is to be sure that one has acquaintance with all the main *kinds* of fields. Specialism is inevitable; but without a comprehensive background it leads to disaster. "Once more the wary glance was shot at me. But he said only, "Of course! And the fields of science are now so many and complex that the scientific background becomes too huge to grasp. However, matters are simplified if one can rule out some great fields as bogus. It is fairly safe to ignore phrenology, astrology, primitive magic, alchemy, religious doctrine, spiritualism and so on; because all that is evidential in them can be satisfactorily incorporated in one or other of the ever-expanding fields of reliable science."

I sipped the last of my sherry, torn between sympathy and revulsion for this hard young mind. I said, "Surely there are some fields in which science is inadequate, some spheres in which, though it can give a very plausible and up to a point useful analysis, yet one can't help feeling that it misses the essence of the matter." "Such as?" "Well, art, moral experience, personal love and what I am tempted to call the living core of religious experience."

"How you cling," he said, "to your illusions! Presumably you don't claim that in the exquisite, almost mystical, bliss of drinking this sherry one must suppose some highfalutin factor that science cannot in principle account for. Then why must you suppose it in art and love and so on?" Laughing, I answered, "Of course in *all* experience there is *something* beyond the reach of science, namely the complete mystery of experience itself; but in some experiences the inadequacy of science is more flagrant than in others. You see, science can approximately describe your sherry-drinking experience in terms of sensation; but in art, love and the core of religion there are factors which contemporary science can neither explain nor adequately describe." Holding his sherry to the light and peering into it with terrier eagerness, he said, "I claim that it *does* describe and explain the one sort of experience as effectively as the other. What it excludes is sheer illusion and superstition. Wine, women and song (meaning all art) and religious excitement can all be explained in terms of innate impulses and Pavlov's great principle of conditioning." Savoring his sherry, he added, "And give me wine, rather than women, because it doesn't make irrational claims on one as they do; and the irrational, sentimental factor in oneself does not stupidly side with it, against one's better judgment." When he had chased the last fragrance of his sherry round his mouth, his lips settled into a pout. Feeling my way, I remarked, "Claims that are irrational to the fundamentally unattached individual may be quite rational where there is genuine love." He expostulated, "Love! Another of those misleading and emotive words! If I love a woman, it is becuase my personality needs intercourse with hers for its fuller expression. Each is food to the other. Neither is really under any sort of obligation to the other, fundamentally, any more than I am under obligation to this soup, or responsible to see that *it* shall express itself fully." "But surely," I said, "you don't suppose that love is just that!" He answered flatly, "Fundamentally, it is just that. But of course it gets overlaid by muddleheaded sentimentality. And of course it is a cooperative affair, and it won't work unless each party shows a good deal of consideration for the other. The profit must be mutual. Further, we have social impulses, and up to a point each individual *needs* to regard the other's interests, and the interests of the little group of two. But fundamentally, each remains an independent and self-interested individual. When a woman claims, as she is apt to do, that each should surrender individuality wholly to the other, that both should drown in the common life, she claims something that it would be quite irrational to give. But the hell of it all is that something in oneself takes sides with her, and in maintaining one's independence one feels inadequate and guilty."

We took our soup in silence. I thought of the love in my own life, of us, of you and me. How easily and plausibly our whole relationship could be stated in his language! And what rare good fortune that each of us should have turned out in the long run to be such life-giving food to the other! In excess, no doubt,

we surfeit each other; and there are elements in each
that the other can never digest. But in the main we
are mutually nourishing.

But presently the thought that, after all, ration-
ally I could not care for you at all save *only* as for my
own person's bread of life, not disinterestedly, not for
your person's intrinsic beauty, and that you also
could care for me only in this self-regarding way, I
found desolating. Surely it debased love to triviality,
and the universe to futility. There must be more to it
than that.

Presently I said, "When there is real love, very
much can be willingly sacrificed for the common life;
and with profit to the individual, though profit is not
the motive. Very much can be sacrificed, but not all,
not one's life work, for instance. But much that was
cherished may be gladly discarded. In love, as in
religion, the primitive, self-absorbed self must be
killed, that a new, more generous self may be born.
And in love the new self is in a way a common self."
He pounced on me. "Sheer superstition!" he said.
"The lovers remain completely distinct individuals.
There is no possibility of a common self." I answered
cautiously, "They remain distinct as centers of
awareness; but if indeed they love (or in so far as
they love, for all lovers are also individualists), each
cherishes the other without thought of profit to his
own individuality. And each cherishes the little
community of two. The common 'we' is felt by both to
be more worthwhile than either of its members."

With asperity he said, "Oh, yes, that does happen.
But the *cause* of this seeming altruism is simply the
fact that each needs the other for self-completion.

The love that is unconscious of its own basic self-regard is silly, sentimental, irrational, neurotic; like a miser caring for money itself instead of the power that money brings. Just so, the silly lover may be conditioned to love the woman herself instead of the limited enrichment that his personality derives from her. We so easily trick ourselves into irrational emotions."

Laughing, I taunted him, "Irrational emotions, apparently, are just those which seem unreasonable from the point of view of your theory that all human behavior is at bottom self-regarding. If you would abandon your theory, you might begin to know what love is."

"Christ!" he said, fiercely cutting at the meat on his plate, "I do know what love is. I was married for love. It was good fun, too. In fact we enjoyed each other immensely. But little by little I found I was too deeply entangled with her. The common 'we' was wrapping me round with a web of subtle spider threads, and sucking the life out of me. I would soon be not myself anymore, but a mere part of that 'we.' It was a pleasant enough process, up to a point; but lethal to *me,* the real, hard, dynamic individual. So long as I was content to be not myself, I was happy in a drowsy, doped way. But sometimes I felt like murder; when she assumed that because I still needed a life of my own, she had failed me, and I did not love her. It was partly my work that she grudged, as something in me that she could not share. Worse, when I showed any interest in other girls, she went all tragic. But I hadn't really changed toward her. I just wanted a bit of variety and refreshment. Well, it was clear to me I must begin cutting the threads. And to my horror I found that I bled at every cut. The irrational sentimentalist in me sided with her, and shrieked with her pain and my own." He looked up at me, and quickly down again. He growled, "Oh, yes! I know love. It's a parasitic disease. It gets into every cell of the body, till there's nothing in one that is the undefiled 'I' anymore. However, I cured myself. I told her we were killing each other, and then I just cleared out, bleeding with love at every pore; but free."

While I was wondering what to say, he began speaking again. "Of course, I soon found I still needed a woman. In the end I cautiously linked up with another girl. I told her straight what I wanted and didn't want; just sexual companionship and no clinging. And she agreed, for she was a scientific worker herself. On this basis we had a lot of fun for a while; but now, hell, she's beginning to want too much. And part of me wants to give it, and to be given it. But once bitten, twice shy. I'm keeping a firm hand on us both, for both our sakes."

Throughout this long confession he had intermittently gobbled his escallop; and I, listening, had forgotten to eat. When his plate was empty, he looked at it with whimsical surprise and exasperation. "Damn!" he said. "It's all gone, and I missed the pleasure of it." We both laughed, and I attacked my food.

Presently I asked my guest to give me a clearer view of that "real, hard, dynamic" individuality of his. What did it really want for itself. "I have told you," he said. "Power, mastery, scientific prestige, a sense of leaving my mark on human society by contributing to human knowledge." Provokingly, I said, "But how irrational! Nothing of this sort is implied in your basic physiological structure. You should be seeking merely chemical equilibrium; and for that end, you should crave merely food, air, water and bodily sexual release of tension. The rest is sheer sentimentality." He laughed. "You can't catch me out that way. Evolutionary forces have given me a conscious nature that needs more than that." I interrupted, warming to my theme. "Much more," I said, "very much more! At every stage of growth we wake to some new range of awareness, become sensitive to some new, subtler features of objective reality; and from the new ranges of objectivity, new values emerge. The child begins to wake from the sheer animal values to the values of personality, prizing the 'I' and the 'you,' and the 'we.' Little by little he discovers society, with all its tangle of conflict and community. Later he may discover humanity, the whole species, with all the values emerging from mankind's long adventure in self-realization in art and science and so on. And finally he may, or he may not, be invaded by the supreme values of, well, of the spirit."

Throughout my monologue, the young scientist had seemingly been interested less in my views than in his fruit flan. But at the word *spirit* he looked at me with the intentness and awkwardness of a dog facing a cat. He said, "You see! Once abandon the attitude of rigorous scientific analysis, nothing prevents you from sliding right down into the slush of religion. From spirit to the Holy Ghost, the Trinity, the Virgin Birth and so on is a fatally easy descent. And what do you *mean* by spirit, anyhow? The word should be abolished."

Challenged, I replied uncertainly, "I mean, not God, not a divine personality, but, well, the ideal way of life that the awakened mind cannot but will, when once this ideal has intruded imperiously into consciousness. I mean the way of intelligence and love and creativity, which, when we are fully awake, we feel to be in some sense what we are *for*." He snorted with indignant triumph, but I continued boldly. "To betray this most lucid intuition is surely to betray something which presents itself to us as sacred. At present we cannot rationalize the experience; but it is far too illuminating and compelling to be denied for the sake of any of our ephemeral theories."

He put down his spoon with emphasis. "Apparently," he said, "you are a confused sort of theist. I prefer the more explicit sort. With them, one knows where one is."

"My point," I said, "is that I know nothing about any kind of Creator or universal personality or God, or about the universe at large, or the status of spirit in the universe. But one thing I do know. What I have called spirit cannot but matter supremely to all conscious beings capable of glimpsing it, wherever in all the wide universe they live. We are animals, yes; but also, in an important sense, we are vessels of the spirit. As for the universe, surely the most appropriate attitude is neither obsequiousness toward a supposed creator nor blind faith that at the heart of it must be love, nor yet the defiant self-pride in humanity, but rather a blend of rapt interest and strict agnosticism. Yet that is not really all. The fully awake human mind must surely feel a kind of dumb piety, an inarticulate worship."

My companion pounced again. He protested, "Piety toward disease germs, worship of blindly destructive natural forces! No! I see no sense in it. Of course, perhaps irrationally, I feel a sort of piety or respect toward the human species, as the most developed thing within our horizon; merely because I have been conditioned by evolutionary forces to respect development. But beyond man, what is there? Just electromagnetic radiation, and the fatal law of entropy. I see nothing admirable in these. Piety toward the universe is just a cock-eyed relic of piety toward its supposed creator; and that, of course, is a relic of the child's respect and fear of the father. No! The adult attitude is to face the universe dispassionately, wary against its brainless power, and quick to snatch advantage from it for one's own and mankind's advancement."

In my turn I protested. "But think! We and the farthest stars are all of the same stuff. If in our tiny bodies it can reach such organization and development, should one not feel a certain awe at the immeasurable potentiality of the cosmos?" He answered, "I, more realistically, regard it merely as a huge field of natural resources awaiting exploitation. Of course, there may be other intelligent species here and there, up and down the galaxies, some perhaps more intelligent than man. But what of it? They are beyond our reach, and I hope we are beyond theirs. If ever we do meet, we shall probably destroy each other. Anyhow, there's our own solar system. Think of the resources awaiting us in the other planets! They will keep us busy for thousands of years, perhaps millions."

Again I protested. "Surely this cult of mere power is trivial. Have Christ and Buddha and the philsophers lived in vain? Can you really have such faith in contemporary scientific ideas? You yourself insist that our science is only provisional and may have to be revolutionized." "Sure!" he answered. "But I can't forestall its development. I must be true to its present findings. Of course, I may extrapolate the course of research a little. I may feel fairly confident that we shall in time possess the whole solar system, or control human inheritance. But I must not open the door to wild superstition and romantic fantasy. To do that would be to betray my most sacred values." "Oh!" I remarked. "So you *have* sacred values?" He answered gravely, "For me personally, intellectual integrity is sacred. But I have no wish to impose my own subjective standards on others."

We sipped our coffee. Betweenwhiles the young man blew perfect smoke rings, projecting some of them through their widening predecessors. He was justifiably proud of this feat; and he enjoyed my smiling admiration.

He said, "I am creating universes, one after another. The primal nebula, each time, is shot into existence from my divine lips, assuming the form they give it. Then it passes through determinate changes, imposed on it by its own physical nature, spawning galaxies of stars, and a few intelligent races. Little by little the law of entropy irons out all differences of potential, freezes out all its intelligences. The frostbound worlds roll aimlessly on. Here and there, maybe, the smothered ruins of a city runcle the snow blanket. Little by little the galaxies disintegrate. The whole universe is dissipated. Meanwhile I have already created its successor."

"A good symbol!" I said. "You should have been a poet." He answered with emphasis, "I prefer more serious work, and better paid."

I remarked that his universes had a creator. "Yes," he said. "And he creates them not in order that they may achieve developed mentality or spiritual awareness or whatnot, but for lack of anything better to do; and perhaps to show off."

At this, a destructive impulse seized him. Scarcely had each annular cloud started on its career when he annihilated it with a wave of his hand.

I suggested that perhaps the great universe itself might also have a creator. "The hypothesis," he said, "is unnecessary. There seems to have been some sort of a beginning to the present order; but before that, probably something like a reverse process held, with contrary natural laws. Anyhow, what matter? We cannot reach back that far. And if there *was* a creator, he must have been less intelligent even than this one. At least, I see no evidence that he had any intelligence at all." I suggested that, if indeed there was in any sense a creator, his intelligence probably so far outranged human intelligence that his purposes and methods would be incomprehensible to us. "Of course!" the young man said, with a smile that was half a sneer. "But that is just fantasy. One might just as well suppose him inferior to us, or that he created merely for the fun of destroying, and tormenting."

Saying this, my cynical friend shattered his last universe, then grimly stubbed out his cigarette. "Look!" he said. "I must go. I have a date. Thanks a lot for the dinner."

A Mystic

I have met a mystic, and now I must tell you about him; a modern mystic, revolted against the modern world.

To fulfill my treasured appointment with him, I was hoisted by elevator to his sky-scraping retreat at the summit of a crag of flats. Strange cell for a contemplative! His room was large and well-equipped. His carpet was moss to the feet; his great chairs, buoyant. On the mantelpiece a small stone Buddha smiled privately in this alien place. On the wall opposite, a Tibetan painting embellished holiness with a wealth of colorful detail. I noted that this treasure did not quite cover the trace of some larger, banished picture. The third wall was books. The eye noted familiar titles of recent literature and of popular scientific works, signposts for the troops and civilians behind the advancing fronts of physics, astronomy, biology, psychology. On the handiest shelf, psychical research jostled with the classics of mysticism. Here, many volumes still wore their dust covers. The fourth wall, all window, revealed as from an aerie the curved and many-bridged, the barge-thronged and tug-disturbed river; an ancient and parasite-infested reptile, gliding through the press of buildings down toward the sea.

Enter the mystic. But could this indeed be he? A spare, stooping figure, his face wan wax, a little sagging; his hair retreating from the global brow and touched with gray; his eyes pale, glacial, but lit (so I told myself) with an interior frosty flame; his lips, though smiling, cheerless; almost, one might say, a child's mouth, but hardened by some adult constraint. He gave me a negligent hand, then sank us both into the chairs. "Cigarettes," he said, "are beside you, if you smoke. I don't."

To make contact, I praised his room. He said, "I used to like it. But now—I have seen through it." To my questioning look, he answered, "Its comforts were a snare, its modish treasures poisoned trinkets. Now, its walls are all diaphanous to reality." I glanced at the great window, but he promptly said, "No! That view also, formerly so stimulating, now jejune, has turned diaphanous; like a pale design on the window itself, too faint to obscure the brilliant, the emphatic reality beyond."

Leaning toward him, I said, "I have often wanted to question you about the reality beyond. I have read your latest book, with admiration, but"—I smiled— "with a certain misgiving." I noticed that he did not respond to my smile. He replied, "To understand it properly, one must first have something of the experience that prompted it." Respectfully I commented, "You, of course, speak with authority, from the experience itself, not from hearsay. But the very clarity of your vision may perhaps make it hard for you to realize some of the difficulties of the novice. One reader, at any rate, cannot be sure whether he himself has something of the experience, or not." The mystic interposed, "If you really had it, you could not doubt; any more than in full sunshine one can doubt the light."

Silently I studied my host: his downcast eyes, his pale soft hands folded in his lap. Could this, I wondered, be indeed a seer? Or was he a mere charlatan, deceiving alike his public and himself? Or was he, perhaps, both seer and charlatan at once? Outraged by our society's vulgarity and heartlessness, had he indeed seen what was lacking, but facilely misdescribed it in terms once vital, now outworn? And this humorless gravity, this self-importance? Could this be compatible with vision?

I said, "Much in your book is echoed in my own experience; but the cosmical meaning, the metaphysical significance, which you find in it, goes far beyond me." With a shade of impatience he answered, "If you had seen clearly, you could not have missed the meaning. The full experience is to be had only after severe discipline, even mortification." "Now there," I protested, "is one of my difficulties. When I tried mortification of the flesh, I felt surprisingly foolish. And far from being freed from self, I became obsessively self-engrossed. Moreover, this violation of the body seemed somehow a treason, a misuse of the spirit's delicate physical instrument. Altogether, that approach I found perverse and rather messy."

The mystic raised his eyes; and the cold fire was for a moment projected against me. But he spoke

quietly. "Mortification," he granted, "is dangerous. It may become an addiction. But where there are more enthralling addictions, mortification of the flesh is the way of life for the spirit. Those who suppose the body's own life to be itself spiritual merely give a fine name to filth, to excuse their wallowing in it." I felt the color rise in my face, but I said nothing, and he remained for a while silent.

Suddenly and surprisingly he extended toward me a deprecating hand, and appeased me with a twisted but a genial smile, accepting me as an equal friend. "I'm sorry," he said. "I was priggish and offensive. I still have to watch myself." This gesture I met with adequate friendliness.

There was again an awkward silence, which at last he broke by saying, "Look! We are getting nowhere. I feel that you are sincere, and if I can I must help you. Let me break the ice by telling you frankly about myself. You probably know that quite recently I was a self-indulgent and futile intellectual. I guzzled pleasures. I gave each impulse free rein. And I secured many little sweet personal triumphs. For instance, I became expert in wine tasting; and I tasted also woman after woman. I was a dilettante in art, and quite an authority on African carvings. But, as you know, my main interest was to figure out the whole pattern of modern culture, and thereby to interpret man to himself. But man was for me nothing but myself writ large, a creature myopic and voracious, caring only to impress his own personality on the universe. For at heart I worshipped only my own exquisite person. Blind to reality, I regarded myself as the most real thing. Godless, I

became my own God; though of course I *named* my
God 'Man.' And how I cherished my freedom, the
freedom of the irresponsible individual! So (how apt
fate's irony!) it was freedom that diabolically enslaved me. The spirit in me was imprisoned,
cramped and crushed within my own blinded, paralyzed, festering, stinking personality. Then little by
little all my pleasures and personal triumphs turned
to dust. I began to be nauseated by my own triviality.
I was seized by an obscure but wholesome yearning
to give myself to something other than me, other
than man; and more admirable. Hitherto, though I
had always some vague perception of such a thing, I
had anxiously, though unwittingly, ignored it. But
now, in the pit of my misery, it revealed itself a little
more clearly. I was sitting in this very chair when I
first glimpsed the truth, about reality and about my
abject self. I was settling down to plan a brilliant and
discreetly devastating review of a rival's book. Suddenly, as though a hand had gently checked me and
swung me round to face in a new direction, I saw that
my intention was trivial and base. I saw it in a new
light. I saw my whole life in a new light. I saw the
difference between the wordly and the spiritual. And
I saw that everything in the universe must be judged
in this new light. Call it the light of the spirit. And in
that light I saw myself as—loathsome. Well, after
that I began to take a firm hand on myself. I
scrutinized my every act, my every motive; denying
my greedy person its filthy satisfactions. But I was
moved to go farther than this. In the past, physical
pain had always been too much for me. I could not
endure it as others endured it, and I saw no reason to

make any effort to do so. But now, I was impelled to use pain for self-mortification. I did not, of course, inflict on myself any extravagant torture. Indeed, I could not have driven myself so far. But the little discomforts and brief torments that I did impose on myself in that early stage were useful. Maybe, for you, who perhaps are not so deeply sunk in filth, they are not necessary."

He was silent, and I wondered whether there was irony in his last remark. Presently I asked if he still continued to practice mortification.

"Not of the flesh," he said, "or only on occasions when the flesh raises its foul head again. By now, I seldom need that first crude discipline. And to practice it longer than is necessary is to succumb to a new addiction. Permanently, the spirit masters the flesh not by mortification but by strict rationing of its pleasures. A horse, once broken in, need never again be thrashed; nor even checked with the curb, but merely with a firm hand on the snaffle. The master may even occasionally encourage it with lumps of sugar, and with comfort in the loose box. But I, though I had broken in the *flesh,* had still to conquer the *self,* to mortify the person. I had strictly to forego those unseemingly personal triumphs, which formerly I had so vaingloriously relished, those vyings with other individuals, ostensibly in service of man, but in fact for sheer masturbatory self-indulgence."

"Surely," I suggested, "you are unfair to yourself. A certain temperate self-satisfaction is justified incidentally, when talents are well used." He answered, "But they were not well used. Personal vaingloriousness, far from being incidental, was my whole aim."

Before I had thought of an answer, he continued. "In another sphere also I have had to mortify the person. There is a woman for whom my untamed self felt not only bodily lust but also personal love. Our natures were complementary and mutually stimulating. Indeed, little by little we had become warp and weft in a single textile. She was for me, if not the only woman, at least the only woman whom I could permanently enjoy. So a little while before I began to see the light, I brought myself to consent to marry her; for I needed to experience (even at some sacrifice) domestic peace and responsible parenthood. But presently, in the dawning light of the spirit I all too clearly saw that this seductive personal accord was itself a snare. I had pursued it merely for its promise of self-increase. Here, therefore, was the supreme opportunity for mortification. Having already foresworn bodily intercourse with her, I now brought myself to foreswear personal intercourse also. I shall now never see her again. Nor shall I see the child whose conception was an added reason for our marriage."

At this point the mystic rose from his chair and paced the room, saying, "It was torture to leave her, and a shock to discover how deeply she had enthralled me. Even now I have not entirely killed my poor self's longing for her. But the struggle has steeled me. It has both clarified my perception of the spirit and strengthened me to consecrate myself single-heartedly to the life of the spirit."

At this moment, I remember, a herring gull sailed indolently past the window on wings that millions of years had perfected, and months in the city had soiled. Its predatory beak and innocently greedy eye were displayed in a brief closeup.

Throughout the mystic's confession I had been torn between respect and revulsion. This heroic self-denial! Yet this fatal self-absorption! I asked myself, did he indeed love the woman, or merely think he loved her? Had he, I wondered, any inkling of what love really is? A surge of horror forced me to speak. "The woman," I said, "the future mother of your child, how she must have suffered!"

Again he subjected me to the frosty flame of his glance; and after a small silence he said, "She agreed entirely that I must at all costs be true to my new calling. For the child's sake we went through the form of marriage; and then we parted. It was, of course, a heavy blow for both of us. And for me it was intensified by natural sympathy for her in her distress. I settled on her practically all my capital, reserving for myself only enough to launch me on the new and starkly frugal life that I had chosen, and shall now very soon begin." He studied my face for a moment, and observing that I was still shocked and perplexed, he smiled. Was it, I asked myself, as friend to equal friend that he smiled? Or was it condescendingly, as one might smile at a child who cannot grasp the solution of some simple puzzle? Gently he said, "My conduct seems to you self-centered, barbarous. Clearly you have not yet gone far in perception of the spirit; and so to you it appears that in abandoning a cherished person I violated something sacred. For we human individuals, you may say, are bound together in unlimited mutual liability. And above all, you may contend, where there is full personal love the obligation is absolute. And so it is, save when the spirit dictates otherwise; as Abraham knew when his God ordered him to sacrifice Isaac. He was confronted with the supreme paradox, namely that at God's command he must do the very thing that God forbids. Having faith, he chose to obey *in virtue of the absurd,* as the greatest of the Danes has said. Absurdly he knew that, since God willed it, all must somehow turn out for the best; even for Isaac."

The mystic stood in silence, with his back to me, and I murmured that I was repelled by so terrible and dangerous an attitude. He faced me. "Terrible, yes," he said, with surprising harshness. "Dangerous, yes! A fatal snare for self-deceivers! But true!"

Then in a milder tone he added, "And think! If I had done this thing for national service or military duty or to immolate myself for some important and dangerous scientific experiment or (if you happen to be a communist) to devote myself to the revolution, you would have joined in the chorus of praise." While I was still wondering whether this was true, he continued, "Well, I did it in order to devote myself wholly to the greatest cause of all, the life of the spirit." The mystic smiled again; and I could not but recognize in his smile a great tenderness; and also a wistful anxiety.

Distressed at my own perplexity, I studied the luxuriant pile of his carpet as I answered, "I do not doubt the sincerity of your devotion, but, well, in the first place I suspect that some of us are apt to sacrifice too readily the immediate and concrete personal obligation to some more doubtful and less urgent, though loftier claim; whether patriotic, social, cultural or whatnot. But let that pass. Clearly there *are* occasions when the beloved must be sacrificed. And I am certainly in no position to judge you. But—" I was at a loss to explain myself. The mystic settled once more in his chair, supporting his chin in his hand, and gazing fixedly at me. Our eyes met once more, and neither flinched. At last I said, "I am daunted by your assurance, by your certainty that your new self-dedication to the spirit is not, after all, self-regarding, and the subtlest snare of all."

Gravely he said, "I know well that spiritual pride is of all sins the most elusive, and the most difficult to eradicate. It is like couch grass interlaced among a rose tree's roots. But there come occasions when we must simply have the courage of our convictions, and face the consequences. Let me put it this way. Only the divine psychologist can know whether in the last analysis my act was true or false. But for me, the situation was in all simplicity this: I heard a call, and I responded. Now if, after all, that call was illusory and my act false, what is the upshot? At the worst, one individual spirit (namely myself) is damned; or rather one very incomplete individualization of the eternal reality is gravely retarded in its age-long search for salvation, or more precisely in the task of self-transcendence and reawakening as the universal spirit; and another individual, namely my wife, is hurt for a few brief months or years. But what are years when we are concerned with eternity? And may she not use this moment of suffering for speedier self-transcendence? On the other hand, if the call was indeed what it seemed, the true and urgent call of the spirit, of reality demanding unconditional service and single-hearted devotion, then my renunciation was right. And I am convinced that this is the case. The spirit calls me, and I must relentlessly obey."

I murmured that I admired his confidence even while I doubted its justification. He answered with startling emphasis, "Good God, man! It's not a case of confidence but stark perception." Then more calmly, "Through fasting and sexual abstinence and mortification, I tell you I *saw* the truth which alone gives meaning to our confused consciousness. And so I *could not but do* as I have done. The truth took hold of me. The spirit dictated to me." "*What* did you see?" I demanded, not without roughness.

He answered promptly, "Fool, how can I tell you what I saw? How can I describe sight to the born-blind?" Then gravely he said, "I saw all time comprised within eternity, all individuals comprised within the eternal individuality, all loves as modes of the eternal spirit, all wisdoms as themes within the ineffable wisdom." Quickly I pounced on him. "Honestly, now, did you really, really see all that?" The mystic was silent, and I waited, while the city's clocks struck the hour. Then slowly a smile of equal brotherhood reconquered his face as he said quietly, "No, I did not really see *all* that. But honestly, honestly, I did *begin* to see. I saw enough to know that such all-redeeming truth *can be seen*. Someday I shall see more."

For a moment his eyes were raised to the little

Buddha, then lowered to his folded hands. The three of us remained silent. Outside, the sad murmur of the city was puncutated by the occasional horns of cars; but within the room silence was a presence. And silence paralyzed my tongue. But my mind still stirred; for I noted that the mystic's expression mimicked the temper of the stone features very faithfully. Was this similarity, I wondered, conscious; or was it the unconscious and spontaneous manifestation of an inner spiritual likeness?

I found courage to speak. "The difference between us," I said, "is perhaps simply that your vision is clearer, and so you are more confident of the spirit's demands on you. But there is one question that I feel bound to ask. As I see it, the life of the spirit is essentially the life of love, of concrete active love of individual persons, and so of active goodwill toward all men. Therefore, what is demanded of us is effective service of the whole terrestrial company of persons. The spirit, as I see it, is not for the isolated individual but for individuals unified in fellowship. Now I can see that we must sometimes sacrifice the immediate concrete personal love to some kind of larger social service. But to sacrifice it to the pure life of the spirit—what does that really *mean?*"

Once more, silence. Presently the mystic spoke again, in a voice that was colorless. I wondered whether this was because he was so held by his vision of high truth that he had little attention to spare for me; or whether his mind was empty as a child's repeating a difficult and imperfectly remembered lesson. "The life of the spirit," he said, "is different for different levels of lucidity. For ordinary unregenerate persons it is simply the way of personal love and honest social service. But on the highest level, the life of the spirit is not action but pure contemplation. Those who are not reborn live in the error that the world of sense perception and action, and of individual persons, is real. They so wallow in the sensuous and the sensual life that it engulfs them. They are as obtuse to the higher ranges of the spirit as an ape to mathematics. Now, I do not contend that the world of the senses is evil in itself. Nothing is evil in itself. But to the spirit in each of us, striving to waken and be the eternal spirit, the world of sensation is a diabolically enticing snare, an exquisitely sweet poison. And the world of persons is equally an illusion and a snare. But through mortification and 'self-naughting' one may reach a state in which not only the whole furniture of earth but also the whole seductive choir of sentient individuals are felt to be a mere clinging mud, holding the spirit down from soaring into its true element. Soon, if one perseveres, the temporal and sensuous veil, with all its bright hard sequins of human individuality, begins to wear thin; and the sequins turn out to be no more than ephemeral sparkles in the universal tissue. At last the phenomenal world becomes little more than a mildly distracting irrelevance; save in so far as it is an imperfectly transparent lens, *through* which reality is to be seen."

Against this view my heart protested, and my reason reached for its trusty weapon of skeptical argument. "But, but—" I said. "Our perceived fellow mortals, to whom you admit we owe a duty of love

and service, must surely be more than phantoms.
How can we owe duty to a phantom? And anyhow,
what adequate reason have you to be so sure that
your seeming vision of ultimate reality is not itself a
mere figment of your own mind, and far more illusory even than the sensed world? I recognize that in
attempting to describe your vision to me you are
bound to falsify it, since human speech is utterly
incapable of signifying what lies wholly beyond the
range of normal experience. And because you can
never describe it to me, I can never appreciate what
it is that you are describing. But there is another,
more serious, difficulty, which, I think, you yourself
have to face. You obviously cannot even *think* about
your vision save by means of human concepts and
therefore human language. Well then, can you be at
all sure that your *interpretation* of your wonderful
vision is not utterly false and sheer illusion; far more
false than the sensed world and the world of concrete
persons?"

He looked at me searchingly before he replied,
"The vision itself can no more be illusion than unin-
terpreted warmth or color or mathematical necessity
can be illusion. The interpretation too, though it
may be profoundly inadequate, *cannot* be false in
essentials. The reality of all else must be judged
solely by the touchstone of the vision. As for concrete
persons, they are of course not *wholly* unreal. They
are illusory only if they are taken to be what they
seem, *self-complete* realities. They are in fact manifestations of the spirit. For that reason, and for no
other, we owe them duty. We, who are ourselves
illusory individuals, are yet real manifestations of

spirit; and as such we are under obligation to those other manifestations over against us in the illusory world of time and physical phenomena. Our separateness is illusory. And this is how it comes that spirit is not for the isolated individual but for individuals together in community." I would have spoken, but he continued, "And as to your skeptical doubt of the hidden reality, I can only repeat that if you had indeed seen, as I have seen, you could not doubt." Again I would have interrupted, but he overbore me with the flow of his own speech. "In the light of the vision it is patently clear why persons matter, and love and all community matter. Persons matter not in their own right but because they are manifestations, very imperfect manifestations, of the universal spirit. And love matters not because it is of service to individual persons, nor yet because it has survival value for society, but because in love spirit. transcends the illusion of separateness, and reaches out to itself in the other. But see! The purest life of the spirit is not in active personal love, though this is indeed the window through which the spirit first appears. The purest life is in contemplation; in contemplation and responsive worship of the spirit itself; culminating in complete self-transcendence. Then comes the eternal moment, the dying of the trivial person, and the waking into the all-embracing eternity of the spirit. It is evident, is it not, that in this supreme experience love itself is transcended. Love is good because in its imperfect way it is a transcendence of individuality in communion with another individual. The Christian 'love of God' is good because it is an obscure yearning for union with the universal spirit. But in the final experience, in the completed transcendence of individuality in the universal spirit, love itself is left far behind; outgrown, in the perfect self-contemplation of the universal spirit."

Ending, he raised his eyes again to mine. Such was their peace that I felt myself to be in the presence of one who had been in the Presence. Yet something in me that I dare not, must not, flout protested insistently against his jargon. Seeing me still in doubt, he smiled, "It is difficult," he said, "to grasp this truth. Well I know how difficult it is for those who are still enthralled by personal love, and dare not outgrow their dearest treasure for the sake of the supreme experience. But the sacrifice is demanded."

How I longed, and how vainly, to know whether this professed mystic was indeed speaking from some all-clarifying experience withheld from me, or whether he had merely bemused himself with too much uncritical reading. How I longed to know whether, in loving you, my best loved of all, I love simply a unique particular being, or (unwittingly) the universal spirit uniquely manifested in you! But indeed, I love you both ways, both for your individual self and as a symbol of the very spirit.

I answered him, "I can see, or at least doubtfully glimpse, truth in your contention. But tell me! (For you have not really answered my question.) If, as you admit, spirit is not for the isolated individual but for individuals in community, is it not essentially for lovers, and in the last resort only for the love-knit community of mankind? And if so, must not the life of the spirit necessarily issue in some sort of social service? If it rejects social service, must it not necessarily be false to itself? Surely, if the individual withdraws from the struggle for a good society in order to seek private salvation in the spirit, he is guilty of treason to the venture of creating a truly spiritual order here on earth. He is no better than a soldier who, at the height of the battle, when every hand is desperately needed, slips away to a quiet place, to enjoy reading the classics of mysticism."

"You are clinging," he said, "to a half-truth. If society is suffering from a mortal sickness, and the cause of the disease is sheer spiritual obtuseness, if society is already tearing itself to pieces in maniacal pursuit of false ends, then clearly the only important social service is for the few elect (who see what is wrong) to segregate themselves for spiritual purification and increase of insight. Later, when the time is ripe, and men are at last sufficiently nauseated by the effects of their own madness, these few elect, or their successors, may return once more to the sick society to become radiating centers of lucidity, and to lead mankind once more toward the light. Or, if it becomes clear to them that the sickness is incurable, then their whole task lies with themselves, namely to advance as far in the spirit as is possible to them."

From some neighboring room in the building came the sound of a girl's laughter. It seemed a sudden, teasing splash of water, with the sun in every drop.

"And which," I asked, "is the case of our world today? Is there hope or are we doomed?"

He answered, "I do not know. The disease is grave. One thing I do know; the time is past for palliatives.

Politics and social reconstruction do not go to the root of the matter. The only hope, and it is a forlorn hope, is spiritual regeneration through the work of a dedicated few. And by now the whole atmosphere of our world is so poisoned that the few must first withdraw themselves for purification. So long as they remain members of a corrupt society, they themselves will remain subtly corrupt. When at last they return, purged and fortified, they *may* be able to save mankind from its own folly. But I doubt it. Human society as it exists today looks doomed, looks damned. Moreover, quite soon a few whiffs of atomic power will probably end man's history. Today, social reconstruction is a repairing of the cabin furniture while the ship is already breaking up on the rocks. On all counts, ours is a time not for works but for faith and prayer."

Did I or did I not catch a faint but unpleasant odor of self-complacency in all this talk? I said, "It is certainly fashionable to say that our present society is damned. And yet I wonder. I have come across so many people who have been shocked by the horrors of our time into a kind of bewildered spiritual shame, a sense that their own lives and other people's have been wrongly orientated. Perhaps, sick as our world is, it is just at the point of turning the corner to recovery."

My host surprised me with a laugh. "When people are badly scared," he said, "they often turn to what they call religion, hoping to save their skins for eternity. But their change is not necessarily a spiritual change at all. It is just a prudential move. No! I see no sign at all of a real spiritual change, save a

steady change for the worse. Having denied the
spirit, and given themselves over to wallowing in the
slime of sense and self, they are blinded and suffo-
cated by their own filthy little persons. They are so
far sunk from spiritual awareness that they idolize
personality, sheer individual selfhood. They affirm
that every individual is an end in himself (whatever
that means), and that the universe is essentially a
place of individual soul making, under a God who is
the supreme person. And in their indulgence in self-
gratulatory worship of individuality, they actually
suppose themselves to have far-reaching spiritual
vision. But this wrong-headed cult of personality,
this idiotic 'personalism,' is a will-o'-the-wisp, sidetracking such feeble spiritual awareness as is current today. As for the masses, they are of course
merely obsessed with bodily pleasure, chiefly sexual,
and the puerile excitements afforded by mechanism.
Their spiritual leaders have betrayed them. They
are hopelessly caught among the cogwheels of the
silly toy that the smart alecks among them have
invented. The press, the cinema, the radio, the aero-
plane and now atomic power are today very effectively destroying man. And what matter? If man is
past saving, the sooner he destroys himself the better. There is at least a satisfactory poetic justice in
his sordid tragedy. He is getting what he deserves,
and getting it in the neck. So to hell with him! Other
worlds and other races will perhaps be better instruments of the spirit; *are* perhaps already so, or have
been so for aeons and aeons."

During this invective I had felt an increasing
discomfort. No doubt mankind was indeed in a sorry

plight; but that the mystic should feel so hotly, so spitefully, about it seemed incongruous. This modern Isaiah, like all his kind, lacked charity. Yes, but a cold voice within me demanded, "Do we, any of us, deserve charity?" At once another, gentler voice replied, "No! Yet to withhold it is to fall short of the spirit."

Something else also seemed lacking in the mystic's attitude. I said, "You condemn the life of the senses as a snare, yet surely in a way, as you yourself have hinted, it is only *through* the life of the senses that spirit can manifest itself. Indeed spirit, so far as I can see, is essentially a way of behaving, not a thing or substance; and for us human beings it is a way of behaving in relation to each other and the whole universe primarily *through* the medium of the physical. And though, of course, we may in some sense kill the spirit by wallowing in sensuality, yet also, for the clearly conscious individual, sense perception and muscular activity may be experienced sacramentally. There is some kind of important truth in the contention that even the humblest physical action, when done 'for the glory of God,' is a spiritual act."

My companion would have interrupted, but I was enjoying myself and would not be checked. His fingers drummed soundlessly on the chair's padded arm.

"You yourself," I said, "must surely have known moments when some sudden gleam of sensuous beauty or some excellence of muscular skill has come with a feeling of religious exercise, as a symbol or epitome of the right relation between individual and

universe. The proportions of a leaf or a bird's wing, a
view of hills and clouds, the accurate thrust of a
spade or the aesthetically right ascent of a rock—
these may sometimes afford a striking experience of,
well, of revelation and of right orientation. No! I
cannot believe that the world of sensation is not a
vehicle of the spirit."

"Oh!" he said. "It is, it assuredly is. But only to
those who constantly look beyond it. If you take it at
its face value, not as a symbol of the spiritual, it
becomes a mere flypaper for the silly buzzing self.
You cannot see it truly and value it rightly till you
have killed in yourself all greedy addiction to it. But
of course, of course, it can be a vehicle of spirit; a
rather crude and gross vehicle, but authentic in its
way, and all we have for setting us in the right
course."

I was appeased, but not wholly satisfied. I said,
"You must surely admit that creative art is among
the highest spiritual activities. And the artist's
whole concern is to make a pattern of sense experiences, a spiritually significant pattern, maybe, but a
pattern to be perceived by the senses."

The mystic looked sharply at me. "In the last
resort," he said, "everything is spirit. There is no
other thing than spirit. But some actualities embody
the universal spirit more completely and signifi-
cantly than others. Art, of course, is a relatively
developed spiritual activity. But it can become a
diabolic snare, when it holds the individual back
from loftier, more deeply spiritual behavior. And
nine times out of ten, that is what it does. Only those
who have outgrown the *snare* of art can see it in true

perspective. The sheer artist can never do so, just because he is enthralled to the sensory. All art, when it is more than a means of self-display or of self-indulgence, is at bottom a childish play activity, a sophisticated doodling with colored shapes, or tones, or the intricacies of verbal association, or the silly undirected dream stuff of the unconscious. Fundamentally, all art lacks seriousness." I glanced at his Tibetan picture, which though it praised the spirit, reveled also in charming intricacies of color and form. The mystic added, "Religious art alone is serious, using the sensory strictly for a spritual end."

I protested that Shakespeare, Bach and Michelangelo did not seem to lack seriousness. He answered, "They play with seriousness, they play with the spirit. For all of them, it's the game that counts. Of course they fulfill a useful function on the highest of the lower levels of experience. They help the weaker brethren to rise beyond the quagmire of mere sensuality and mere utilitarian praxis. But so long as the artists remain mere artists, their whole attitude is at bottom (from the more lucidly spiritual point of view) frivolous."

This arrogant condemnation so bewildered me that for some while I remained silent. But even while I condemned it as insensitive and complacent, I was teased by a suspicion that, in the light of some experience withheld from me, there might nevertheless be a truth in it. Indeed, even I had some disturbing glimmer of that light.

However, I could not help being outraged by the mystic's calm rejection of the existing world of men. Or was the secret source of my exasperation no more than resentment at his assurance, and at the disturbing possibility that he had indeed seen the glory that I should never see? Churlishly I remarked, "So you intend to wash your hands of us all and let us stew in our own juice while you save yourself." "Yes," he answered, firmly but with a most unexpected twinkle in his frosty eyes. Then he voiced a thought that I had refrained from expressing. "I shall be a rat with the sense to leave the sinking ship." I asked how he intended to escape, and how he would disinfect himself of all taint of us.

"You feel indignant," he answered, smiling with one of his odd gleams of friendliness, "but believe me I am not seeking mere personal salvation. I am simply loyal to the dictates of the spirit. I shall withdraw, hoping to return, strengthened for helping. What I shall do, along with others, is the only possible way to save mankind. You probably know that groups of the dedicated have already been founded. I am not satisfied with any of them, so I am planning to found (along with others who feel as I do) a minute community dedicated to the spirit, and far out of reach of the modern world's infection."

I could not resist saying, "It sounds like Shangri-la." He answered rather wearily, "It does, of course. But this is the real thing, and no mere fantasy."

I asked him how his community would maintain itself alive. "Some of us," he said, "are farmers, some craftsmen. All of us can work. We are buying land in a remote but temperate country. A few of us are experienced writers. We shall not hesitate to use our art for the twofold purpose of spreading the truth and eking out our slender livelihood."

Surprised, I ejaculated that to do this must surely involve continued commerce with the wicked world. He answered, "The printed word and royalties are the modern equivalent of the mendicant friar's preaching and receipt of alms."

Cynical thoughts occurred to me, but I said only, "How on earth did you catch your farmers and craftsmen?" Still amiably, he answered, "Countrymen, you know, are often nearer to the spirit than townspeople. We have found among the many who are blind a few who at least are groping. As to status, our new friends will of course be equal to us in brotherhood. In practical matters they will be our masters, but in spiritual matters leadership will be ours, since we shall be the recognized interpreters of the spirit."

A laugh escaped me; but he said, "You are cynical, because you have not access to the experience that unites us all in spiritual brotherhood."

The mystic told me a good deal more about his projected community, but I did not attend very carefully, for I was anxiously and vainly debating with myself as to whether he was authentic. So much in his character and his attitude seemed unlovely; but a new and deeper awareness seemed striving to transform him.

I had risen and gone over to the great window to look more closely at the unhappy world that he was renouncing. The crowded roofs were a sea of tumbled lava, or the puckered crust of some insect's teeming comb. They extended in all directions to the horizon, spiked here and there by spires and factory chim-

neys. Beneath each covering of slate or tile the little
personal creatures were probably everywhere
scheming to snatch some particular joy. And everywhere the sick world either withheld the prize entirely or yielded it up infected with the universal
plague. Across the river, giant posters blared of beer
and whisky, lipstick and laxatives. In the nearby
railway station a locomotive, starting, snored suc-
cessive columns of steam unto the still air. Each
mushroomed slowly. Below me, by the river, cars
were bound on their thousand trivial or self-impor-
tant errands. Idlers leaned over the river wall,
watching the freighted barges, the pleasure steam-
ers, the gulls, which from my lookout were mere
grimy snowflakes. A public lawn was starred and
crescented with flower beds. Voices of playing children pierced the snarl of the traffic with sparkles of
sound. Lovers, minute as pairing chromosomes, lay
full-length together. Prisoners of war, demolishing
an old air-raid shelter, were ants, enslaved by an
alien species. They bore witness to our world's dis-
unity, and to our heartlessness. On a nearby building, the flag of island freedom, but also of imperial
tyranny, mocked their slavery.

Presently I noticed that many faces were turned
upward. Following the direction of their gaze, I saw,
high on the steel skeleton of a burnt-out building, a
tall crane. And on its crest a man was straddled, air-
surrounded, his feet dangling in the sky. Leaning
forward and downward, like a horseman sabering
foot soldiers, he was battering with a great hammer
on stubborn metal almost beyond his reach. The bare
muscles of his shoulders glistened with sweat. Be-

low, the upturned faces waited, held by vicarious fear, or by admiration, or the unacknowledged lust to see him fall.

This whole world of massed human individuals grappling with the physical, would soon be abandoned by my companion, and with little regret. Idlers, toilers, children, lovers and that sweating Thor riding on the machine were for him all damned, because all enthralled by the physical. And though he payed homage to love, he felt (or so I guessed) no warmth of compassion for this doomed city, this doomed world. How could it be otherwise? One does not pity a shadow. And all this was for him but a shadow, a veil of illusion drawn between him and the reality for which he yearned.

I could not wholly doubt that the mystic had experienced some deep significant fact. Indeed, in my hesitant way I too had experienced something of it. But though logically his withdrawal might, I told myself, be justified by his supreme experience, I was repelled by his readiness to abandon the damned to their fate. Spirit, we had agreed, was for individuals in community. To withdraw from the concrete community which gave one individual being, even to withdraw for the sake of a future and better community, or even for the sake of the pure spirit itself, smacked of desertion. My heart protested, if our world is damned, let us all be damned together! And yet I had to admit that if his vision was indeed authentic and rightly interpreted, his course was right. And yet, and yet ... This yearning for the reality behind appearance, this readiness to sacrifice the actual to the ideal, smacks unpleasantly of the blind old cult of progress, and faith in a far off millennium. That the heaven is to be had here and now, and eternally, makes no difference. Cosmical piety dictates that I, a finite and ephemeral being, shall not lust even for union with God or the universal spirit. If at heart, though unwittingly, I have that unity all the while, well, it is so. But to lust for it is surely an addiction, a greed, and the subtlest betrayal of the spirit. Rather, "my station and its duties."

But the mystic would reply, and not without reason, that this craving for union with God or the Whole was not a mere individual's craving; it was the urge of God in him to wake wholly to his godhead.

Well, let each of us be true to his own light. But for me there must be no withdrawal. Let me live somehow in the two world at once. Immersed in the temporal, let me nonetheless look with a far-seeing or an inner gaze on the eternal. Let me indeed see the eternal; but I must find it *within* the temporal, not beyond. The grit and hardness of the rock under the climber's fingers are not phantom. If he thinks them so, he is lost. Yes, and his goal is no cosmical panorama from a summit perhaps inaccessible; his goal is the climbing; to adapt himself, body and mind to objective reality, and thereby to express the spirit in him. This; but also (in sidelong glances only) to be as aware as may be of the depth below and the sky above, and the whole horizon of mountains. This, surely, is the truth that you and I together have conceived, each contributing. Is it not so?

I found that the mystic had left his chair and was standing beside me, considering my face, and smiling. "My way," he said, "is not yours; and yours, not mine. Be true to your own light, as I shall be to mine. There is a place for both our kinds."

Gently, he took my arm and led me to the door.

A Revolutionary

I have met a formidable young man, a revolutionary, and I must tell you about him.

I had left the car in the ditch with its bent front axle. (How machinery can fetter us, not only by its promise of ease and power but also by its helplessness when broken!) A passing lorry brought me to the town. The first garage refused the salvage, being shorthanded. The second offered to bring the car in at once and to repair it next week. And there was I with my engagement next morning and my journey scarcely begun! The third also refused; but in the end the boss, a genial creature, clumsily acting the part of a go-getter, agreed to spare me one man on condition that I myself, since I claimed to be not entirely without experience, should work as his (unskilled) assistant.

A pale young mechanic was summoned. He had a slight limp and the face of a nun; or perhaps rather an abbess, for it combined purity and authority. His challenging eye surprised me with an occasional sharp twitch of the eyelid, which at first I mistook for a wink. His hair, plastered but unruly, had broken

rank. A heavy lock drooped over his brow. I thought
of the trailed wing of a damaged bird. Raven, I
wondered, or jackdaw? And was the hurt actual, I
foolishly wondered, or feigned to distract strangers
from some secret treasure? He regarded me as
though passing a private and unfavorable judgment
on me, glancing at my hands. My smile won no
response.

Presently we were in the breakdown lorry, with its
crane, a megatherian but jaunty tail cocked up
behind. A sparrow perched for a moment on its crest,
but took wing when we started. To make conversation, I told about the accident, explaining that apparently the steering gear had broken. The mechanic said only, "We shall see." And without
shifting his eyes from the road he winked, or so it
seemed. Perplexed and disconcerted by his tacitur-
nity, I apologized for fetching him out in filthy
weather. He answered, "I'm paid for it."

When we had reached the crippled car, he expertly
examined the trouble, while I put on my overalls.
Presently he said, "Steering seized up and broken.
Steering-arm bolt sheered. The joint has been
parched for oil." His raised eyebrows censured me.

When the crane had been maneuvered into position, my companion crouched on the wet grass to fix
the chain for lifting the front of the car. I stood by,
willing but unhelpful; gloomily studying the scurf in
the young man's hair, and a gnat that had lost itself
in that black jungle. After a good deal of manipulation and removal of obstacles, he succeeded in loop-
ing the chain round the axle; then he invited me to

turn the windlass of the crane while he kept an eye on the car's hoisted head. The wheels were soon free of the ground, and we swung the crippled vehicle round into line for towing. The mechanic mounted the lorry's driving seat. I took up my position beside him, producing cigarettes.

On the slow journey to the garage I attempted several gambits of conversation, from the weather to politics, from the flicks to the economic crisis. His responses were perfunctory and brief. At last I challenged him on more intimate ground. "Do you *like* your job? It must be tiring, but it's good skilled work, and socially useful." He laughed sourly. Then after a pause he said, "It's all right." I did not pursue the matter. It was as though I had been vainly knocking at a shut door in a shabby street; suspecting, moreover, that I had caught sight of someone watching through curtains.

In the garage, with its hum of machinery, clatter of metal, smell of exhaust gases, and an occasional splutter of curses from a mechanic at work under a nearby car, we set about dismantling the axle.

I must tell you about the work in some detail, even if it wearies you, because I cannot give the man without his environment; and the main feature of his environment was the all-pervading and exacting presence of mechanism; of sick machines, which imposed trains of meticulous activity upon their human doctors and nurses.

Our task, for instance, was quite a complicated one; and I soon found that in the twenty-five years since I had tackled this sort of thing techniques had

changed. We had to take off the two front wheels, disconnect the track rod, remove the damaged bolt from the steering arm, and substitute a new one. Then came the operation of relieving the axle of its two stub axles, those great hinges on which the wheels turn sideways for steering. Finally, we had to unscrew the four stirrup bolts that hold the axle to the two front springs. Then at last we should be able to undertake the job of straightening the axle. There was also a damaged wing to be roughly repaired.

I regarded the operations ahead of us with exasperation and gloom, for to me they were just an irrelevance. But my companion attacked the work with quiet relish, or so I inferred from his loving way of handling the tools, and a certain firm delicacy and rhythm in all his actions.

While he worked on one side of the car, I hesitantly and clumsily attacked the corresponding member on the other side. He, of course, was always ahead of me. Sometimes, if he saw I was in difficulty, he would come round to help me. Once, when I felt him watching my awkward movements, I was flustered and let my spanner slip, barking my knuckles. To my surprise he said, consolingly, "Bad luck! The best of us do that sometimes." Then he added, with a new friendliness, which however was salted with sarcasm, "You don't handle the tools *quite* like a novice. Learned the tricks of the trade on your own car, I suppose?" I told him vaguely that I had spent most of the First War on cars, and a short spell in a workshop. He made no comment.

Well, after a lot of struggling and sweating on my part we had the freed members all parked by the garage wall, and the mutilated front of the car looking rather like a skull with no lower jaw. We also removed the crumpled wing; and then we carried the axle to the forge and settled it snugly into the coals. I, unbidden, took charge of the bellows, while my colleague piled on more fuel and made ready the blacksmith's tools. Then he waited, and we both watched the rhythmically increasing glow. Producing from within his overalls a small green packet, he offered me a cigarette. I said, "I don't seem to have much wind to spare at the moment." But I accepted the fag, and put it behind my ear. I saw him smile to himself at this too consciously proletarian gesture. Then, taking a long pair of pincers, he picked out a bright coal and lit his own cigarette. For some time he watched me critically. Presently he said, "You have forgotten the trick. Don't work so hard at it. Let her keep her own rhythm." I slowed down; but my action remained awkward, for I was self-conscious under his scrutiny. Presently he relieved me at the bellows, and we both smoked.

Anxious to seem thoroughly at ease, I remarked brightly that I was rather enjoying myself as a garage hand. He replied, "Just as well, since you're not paid for the job." Uncertainly, I said something to the effect that it was good practical skilled work, and that watching him I couldn't help feeling he enjoyed it himself. To this he answered rather violently, "If you had to stick to it all day and every day, you'd soon get fed up with the whole bloody life."

I was disconcerted by the note of anger in his voice. To my clumsy reminder that he had said his work was "all right," he answered, "At bottom *it's* all right, and it might be grand, but—" He eyed me as though debating whether to be frank or not, but remained silent. I queried, "Conditions bad?" "Good enough," he said, "but, well, *society* makes the whole thing all wrong." To my silly grunt of sympathy he replied hastily, "Oh, I'm well enough fixed up myself, really. The boss is all right, as they go. Might be a real good sort if it weren't for his false position, as employer. The pay gives me all I need, for the present. But, hell, what's it all *for,* the work, I mean? You said it was socially useful work, and so it might be. But the actual aim, naturally, is just to put money in *his* pocket, and to—" When I goaded him to go on, he said with sudden rage, "To help people like you with plenty of money to waste society's petrol on amusing themselves."

He looked at me with the cold gaze of a duelist who has drawn blood and is ready to parry the counter-stroke. But I merely laughed off my small wound and said, "I see." He continued to oppose me with his rapier glance, and presently he said, quietly, "You might get me sacked for that." "That way," I said, "I should earn the contempt of a man I respect. Even if we *are* on opposite sides of the class war, which we're not really, we can treat each other with the respect due from person to person." He threw the butt of his fag into the forge. "Persons!" he snorted. "Cells in a sick society, nothing more! We are determined through and through by our social conditioning, and mainly by the thought forms imposed on us by the economic circumstances of the particular class to which each of us belongs." Once more the wink. He added, "Of course it's not really your *fault* you're a cell in the cancer lump; nor any credit to me that I am a humble muscle cell, and relatively sound." Again the wink.

By now, however, I was beginning to tumble to it that his prodigious wink was involuntary. All the same, I had a strong feeling that in some way it was significant, though unconsciously. Throughout my dealings with him his false wink falsely gave the lie to his manifest sincerity, and falsely invited me to laugh at his most treasured convictions. It was as though, deep within him, some buried self were humorously and forlornly signaling behind the other's upright back.

At this point he deserted the bellows for a moment to readjust the axle's position in the forge. He turned it over. The part that had been submerged in the coals was already dimly glowing.

When I could turn my attention from considering his eyelid's queer behavior, I said, "You think we are wholly shaped by our class ideology, but what about Lenin? He was a lawyer, not an artisan, yet it was he that led the worker's revolution."

My companion embarked on a harangue. He even forgot to work the bellows, so I silently took his place. "Yes," he said, "the more alert among the bourgeoisie sometimes react not merely to the circumstances of their own class but to society as a whole. For the workers, of course, there's really no conflict, since the interest of *their* class is identical with the interest of society. But you comfortable people find it almost impossible to see beyond your own noses, or rather beyond the interest of your own reactionary class. The few who do succeed have all had some shock or other to wake them; like Lenin, who was outraged by the government's murder of his brother. Even so, we find that all but the very great ones (like Lenin) remain hidebound by their class ideology. At heart, you see, they never really get beyond being mere liberals. When it comes to the point, they funk the revolution, on the plea of forbearance, or Christian charity, or the inevitablity of gradualism. And so they do more harm than good."

I remarked to my companion, with a sarcasm that failed to touch him, that he seemed to know all about it. He answered, quietly, "I read the one newspaper that champions the workers; and I watch people. In fact I keep my eyes open. And the great revolutionary writers help me to understand what I see." I asked him if he was quite sure that they themselves understood, in any deep way. Without taking his eyes from the axle, he said, "They explain human behavior realistically, in terms of the economic motive; and in the long run this is all that counts, for the understanding of history. This goes deep enough for anyone who is concerned with social action." Once more the wink attacked him, and he impatiently rubbed his eye with his bent forefinger. I pointed out that the workers were far from being united in favor of the revolution which was to put their class in power. "Of course," he said, with an impatient glance at me. "Of course! They're hampered in two ways: by sheer blind stupidity, which prevents their seeing through the smoke screen of capitalist propaganda to the true interest of their class; and by antisocial self-interest. For the sake of individualistic dreams they betray society by violating their own social nature. You see, in the last resort the fully enlightened self-interest needs must identify itself with the interest of society; and so with the interest of the working class, which *is* the interest of society. Maliciously, I added, "In fact the only way to personal salvation is to recognize that we are all members one of another, and to live whole-heartedly for love." I chuckled. "Put it that way if it amuses you," he said, "but I prefer more scientific language. It's more precise and less misleading. Love is just a subjective emotion due to glands and so on. For action one must think in terms of objective historical forces."

I protested that even expert historians disagreed violently about historical forces. "You're right," he said, emphatically. "It's because they can't see the wood for the trees. At one time, when I was little more than a raw adolescent, I had a craze for attending evening classes. Specially after the military had refused me because of my stiff ankle. I felt I wanted something to live for, so I decided to live for the truth." He laughed at himself. "I began with a course on history and found Henry Ford was not far wrong when he said history was bunk. *That* sort of history *was* bunk. I also tackled psychology, thinking it would go deeper. In a way it did; but it didn't help me to understand the social mess; and it was *social* truth I wanted. I even began on philosophy; but, hell, it was all just playing with words. At last I tried a course in economics. The tutor seemed very worried about one Karl Marx, so I started reading Marx on my own. That introduced me to a new sort of economics and history; yes, and philosophy, too. It all made sense, fell into a pattern. Of course I realize now that old Marx is not infallible. But he's dry and scientific and unsentimental. And he gives you something big to live for and fight for."

At this point sunlight broke through the murky garage window and lit up countless motes in the air, so that a wide slanting shaft of light reached to the forge, turning fierce coal and axle into a mildly radiant living thing, into a glowing heart of love. The mechanic, a half-seen ministering figure, bowed over this tender being, his nun's face lit from below by its radiance. The rest was darkness. Then the sunlight vanished and with it that strange nativity.

The young man now put on more fuel, and then relieved me at the bellows, saying simply, "My turn, now."

Presently my mind reverted to a phrase that he had casually used. I said, "About this 'illusion of individuality'? What do you really mean? After all, you and I aren't illusions, are we! Individual conscious beings do exist, don't they? There's no denying that. And the state, thank God, is not an overmind." He answered with a teacher's patience, "Yes, but the individual is not a tight little pea rolling about on a plate with other peas. He's just a node in the social tissue, just a knot in the great net of society. Without society he's nothing. (How do they put it?) He's a focal point where social forces determine consciousness. Of course society is just made up of individuals, as a net is made up of knots; but it's society that matters; the net, not the knots." Against this view I protested. I said I could understand the view that *nothing* mattered, but that society, as such, should matter, rather than individuals, seemed to me a crazy notion.

Thinking of you and me, of our long growing-together, with its joys and pains (its growing pains), I had a sudden ridiculous vision of your face all puckered with amused exasperation when the milk boiled over before you could reach it. How could the loved individual behind that face not matter, I said to myself, inwardly laughing.

But aloud I said only, "Surely, surely, it's people that matter, and loving some of them. Yes, and all the workings of creative imagination and creative intelligence. All *these* matter, absolutely. And nothing else."

For a moment my companion paused in his work, and I seemed to hear a tremor in the breath that he took. Gently he said, "You have got it all wrong, comrade." (The word had slipped out, and he smiled at his mistake.) *"Nothing* matters absolutely. Good and bad are relevant to human wants. And of course what we all want is happiness, and to love and all that. But when you begin to understand historical forces, you find you don't want the old sort of happiness (personal success and love and so on); you want happiness for mankind as a whole. You discover that what matters for you is not just yourself, not even Tom, Dick and Harry, or *all* selves, but the whole social *tissue* of individuals. Each of us matters only insofar as he fulfills a useful function in the whole." Interrupting, I demanded, "And what is 'useful'?"

For some moments he was silent, staring somberly

at the forge. Then he said, with some exasperation, "We all know well enough what is useful, because we all know what it feels like to be frustrated. At any rate, the workers do." This answer did not satisfy me. I said, "But when the revolution has done away with social frustration, *then* what is useful?" Again he fell silent. Then he answered, dully, "That's really a false question, because we can't imagine ourselves into that time. New needs will always arise with the increasing complexity of society. But presumably, in the last analysis, what is useful is whatever is needed for fulfilling the dynamic potentialities of society. These include cultural activities like art and science, but the final sanction seems to be just power to dominate the nonhuman environment, power to organize the whole world for human living."

When I protested against this lame conclusion he answered hotly that the whole question was purely theoretical and sidetracking, and couldn't be answered in any significant way. Then he turned from defense to attack. "Anyhow," he said, "what sort of answer is yours? You say individuals matter. They do, to themselves, and sometimes to each other. But seen in a wider context, seen from the point of view of society, seen objectively, they don't matter in themselves at all. From the point of view of the hive, the individual bees are mere organs, mere cells in the social tissue. If we were not *essentially* social by nature, expressions of the social environment, there might be some point in each one's trying to be a perfect little flower of personality, like a woman caring only for her own beauty, and for admiration.

But, Christ, how dull, how bloody dull that sort of thing is! And since we *are* social, how mean and evil it is too, in the only true sense of the words."

Without a pause he said, with a roughness that was at once exasperated and genial, "Come on, mate, this thing is about cooked now. Quick! Give me a hand."

We seized the axle with long pincers and lifted it from the forge. The crooked region glowed like a bar of sunset. Its surface was sprinkled with brighter sparkles. We fixed one cold end in a vice and tugged at the other with levers, to straighten the glowing crook. Conversation ceased. We strained and sweated; but the brightness faded to a ruddy gray before the main bend was even roughly straightened. My companion let go, remarking, "The bugger'll have to be cooked again. Come on, we'll give him hell this time, comrade." We both laughed, and I said, "Right, comrade! We'll liquidate the stiff-necked reactionary." We carried the axle back to the forge, and again I took up my place at the bellows, while he settled the bend snugly into the red hell and put on more coal.

I challenged him. "What *sort* of a revolution is it that you want, and are presumably working for?" He seemed to be musing, for he ignored my question. I repeated it. Still musing, he said, "Of course an easygoing revolution would be pleasantest; but no ruling class ever gives up without a struggle, so probably there'll be bloodshed. As soon as the government brings itself to do something really revolutionary the bosses will begin to take action with tanks and machine guns. And then, of course, they will have to be brought to heel with superior force. But of course the government may not ever do anything revolutionary." He fell silent, but when I prompted him, he said, "Then a resolute minority, knowing the need of the people better than they do themselves, may have to seize power. And if America tries to stop them, Russia will help them."

"Good God!" I said, laughing uneasily. "You're a dangerous fellow! So the resolute and far-seeing minority are actually to force the masses to have what is good for them, even at the risk of a world war."

He came to with a jerk. "Hell!" he said. "I meant it all in the abstract, of course. How did you get me talking this way?" I eagerly explained that he was talking this way because we had made a real personal contact, and so we couldn't help trusting each other. He staged a bitter laugh, and said, "Trust you? You're one of them, not one of us. I have no reason to trust you at all. You may be a bloody spy for all I know." The wink closed his eye for a full second.

In silence we both watched the brightness of the forge wax and wane in time with the bellows. Once more the axle became a bar of sunset. I suggested that we might now complete the bending, but he said, "No! It's still only orange; we must bring it up to primrose if we can." I redoubled my effort. Sweat streamed into my eyes and was salt in my mouth. "Let me have a turn," he said. And as we changed he gave me a child's shy smile. After we had put in a little more strenuous work on the bellows, the axle achieved a dazzling brilliance. "Now!" he said; and we hastily set it once more in the vice. Once more we levered and tugged, till he was satisfied that the true shape was restored. Then we took the axle to the anvil; and while I held it in position or turned it according to his orders, he gave the final touches with a hammer. The trailed wing of his forelock quivered with each blow. His pale face glistened with sweat. Presently he flung the hammer aside, saying, "That'll have to do. The thing's as stiff as a corpse again." He straightened himself, wiped his sweating hands on some waste, and blew a droplet from the tip of his nose. Our eyes met, and he grinned with schoolboy satisfaction. He said, "If only we could make the new world that way, with anvil and hammer, instead of machine guns, and people squealing in pain! But what history demands, must be." "Rot!" I retorted, as we laid the axle aside to cool.

This was the moment when I burnt my wrist. I grazed it against the hot axle and let out a yell. I apologized for my clumsiness and assured him that the hurt was nothing. In a moment my companion was transformed into a sister of mercy. Taking hold of my forearm with gentle hands, he examined the burn; and a surprising little cry of sympathy escaped him. Then with a motherly tenderness that I found embarrassing, for the hurt was indeed trivial, he murmured comforting words as though to a child that had bruised himself. He hurried away and returned with a first-aid outfit. He washed his hands in a tin basin with "Gresolvent," and then with carbolic soap. Soon he was applying some ointment or other to my wrist. Lint followed, and cotton wool. Then with firm but delicate touch he wound a bandage round the wrist and through the fork of the thumb. Expertly he divided the end of the bandage and knotted the two strands round the wrist, with the knot well away from the damage. He laid a caressing hand for a moment on the finished work. The gesture combined tenderness and pride in artistry. "That'll be all right," he said, "but don't use it too much for a bit." It was as though he were a great surgeon examining a patient recovering from some ticklish and successful operation. Our eyes met, and he must have seen my embarrassment, for he said, apologetically, "One can't be too careful," and added, "I wish I could have been a doctor."

Turning brusquely from me, he drew from an inner pocket a large old watch on a strap, and ejaculated, "Jees! It's dinnertime." I asked him to be my guest at a meal, but he refused with some return of hostility. He insisted on washing my hands for me. We took off our overalls; and as he seemed to be dawdling impatiently I tactfully left him.

After the gloom of the garage, my eyes contracted to cope with sunlight. The air sparkled with a shower of diamonds. The wet street gleamed. The tawdry facades displayed a real though borrowed glory. For even a poor little north country work town can be transfigured by celestial stagecraft to suggest the New Jerusalem. The faces of the people, homely but sunlit and freshened, adequately simulated pilgrims newly arrived in heaven. Their terrestrial clothing, their shawls, cloth caps, frayed mackintoshes and wrinkled or laddered stockings had still to be transmuted into the raiment of the blessed, but they had arrived in heaven. Closer inspection shattered the illusion. A policeman was admonishing a peddler. An old beggar held out a cap containing a nest-egg penny. A queue waited for rations. A news vendor displayed a poster announcing "The Atom and Russia."

Presently a more pleasing vision attracted me. A girl was distributing leaflets. She was a gallant little figure in gray trousers and a scarlet waterproof jerkin. Her dark hair, a halo in negative, gleamed with raindrops. With every leaflet she gave also a smile such that no man could resist, and surely no woman either. Some recipients of her literature studied it with care; some, after a mere glance, crumpled it and impatiently threw it into the gutter. As I approached, she encountered a woman carrying a baby in her shawl. I was following in the mother's wake, and I saw the young amazon's smile change. When my turn came and I was reaching out my hand for the leaflet, our eyes met; and for an instant, before the appropriate gaiety was restored, I was arrested by the depth of sorrow in that young face, so that I did not at once take hold of the paper. She pushed it into my hand, wrinkled her nose at me, reconstructed the smile, and turned for the next victim. Walking away, I read, "Protest meeting against dismissal of strikers," and so on. I put the leaflet in my pocket and continued my search for an eating place.

When my solitary meal was over, I hurried back toward the garage. Presently I found that I was overtaking a linked couple. There was no mistaking the red jerkin and the dark orb of hair. As I drew nearer I recognized that the man was my mechanic. He was talking earnestly to her, and from time to time I saw his ascetic profile lit with love. I slowed my pace and turned into a side street to allow them to reach the garage before me.

When I arrived, the young man was already at work. He had fixed the car's damaged wing on a bench and was carefully flattening out the puckers with a lead mallet. His smile of greeting was genial. He said with mock censure, "You're late! You'll be losing your job." Then he deserted the wing, and together we carried the cooled axle to the car, propped it roughly in position with blocks of wood, and began to refit the stirrup bolts. We worked in silence for a while, my companion seeming disinclined to talk. But his silence was not hostile, as it had been earlier in the day. My mind's antennae reported him as friendly, but absorbed.

When the axle was fixed, we attended to the steering arm. The sheered bolt had to be driven out of the socket with a punch and hammer, for rust had gripped it. When this was done, he cleaned the socket and oiled it, and lifted the whole stub axle back to the car to fit it in position once more. I followed suit with the other one. We inserted the bolts of the track rod. I was working at high pressure to keep pace with the more skilled man, but he said, "Take it easy, mate! You have a damaged wrist. I'll do the final tightening, to save your straining." This he did; and when the job was finished, he kept pushing the whole mechanism to and fro on its hinges as though anxiously testing the steering. But

I could see that he was absorbed in his own thoughts.

Presently, without raising his eyes, he said, "You think I'm heartless about individuals, but I'm not. My trouble is that I am far too much tangled up with individuals. I'm not *really* 'possessed' by the revolution, as some of the comrades are. I try to be, but I can't be; not really." I waited for him to continue; and after a long pause he said, "Of course I *do* whatever has to be done. I have a reputation to keep up. But I have to force myself all the time. Outwardly I'm the leader, and they say I'm steel-willed. Inwardly I'm *quite* different. How Lenin would despise me! And because I know he would, I have to drive myself harder and harder. And that makes me drive the comrades hard, too. Sometimes they grumble, sometimes they slack, but I can always kick them into action again."

He rose, and fetched one of the wheels, and began to work it into position on a stub axle. I dealt with the other; in silence, for his confession intrigued me. But he did not continue it, till I had said, "Tell me more, if you feel like it." Presently he said, solemnly, "I have a girl friend." For a moment he looked at me across the front of the car with the eyes of a nesting bird on its eggs. He continued, "*She's* the real thing all right. She's heart and soul for the revolution. Together we really are a fighting unit. They call us the master cell. And if I drive the comrades, it's she that drives me. Just by believing in me, and setting me an example. Christ! I've *got* to live up to her belief in me." He was tightening up the wheel with fierce though accurate strokes of the lead mallet. Then he said, "But of course that's the wrong motive.

I mustn't do it for *her*, but simply for the revolution. Perhaps I ought to give her up. Fancy *her* being a snare!"

I interrupted. "Good God, man! You're no revolutionary. You are just a puritan absorbed in your own struggle for righteousness, for salvation. As a Marxist you must believe that what matters is action, not motives. And you say that in action you're sound."

He said nothing.

Both wheels were fixed. He fetched a long-handled jack to lever the car's weight from the blocks, so that I could move them away. Then he lowered the car till the wheels once more touched the ground, and the tires flattened very slightly with the car's weight.

He said, "In a way you're right, of course. But the point is, I'm dependent on her. As a unit we're sound in action, but without her I probably couldn't keep it up." After a pause he added, shyly, "You see, for me she *is* the revolution, the spirit of the revolution, concentrated in one little girl. That's really why I love her." His eye emphatically winked. "So, after all, if I act from her belief in me I really am acting from loyalty to the revolution, to the spirit of the revolution embodied in her." His eyelid flickered, and I let out a guffaw. "That's not much like Marxism," I said. He flushed and answered sharply, "It's quite sound, really. I didn't use Marxist language, but what I meant was just that historical forces have made her into the ideal comrade in revolutionary work, and that I want to cooperate with her all my life."

This was too much for me. I laughed again, and so far forgot myself as to give him a friendly punch, from which he recoiled with dignity. "Good God!" I said. "Can't you admit you're in love with the girl herself? Marxism is all very well, but if you push it too far it turns just silly. Human beings are very complicated things. They live in several dimensions at once, not just in one. And if they try to live just in one, they warp themselves horribly. Besides, if the revolution is controlled by one-dimensional minds, *it* will be warped too, horribly. If you go on the way you are going now, you'll grow into a dangerous fanatic; and if dangerous fanatics guide the revolution the whole thing will be poisoned. Instead of being inspired by love it will be harsh and barbarous and deadly."

He had been standing idly, wiping his hands on a bit of waste. Now he turned away brusquely to continue work on the damaged wing. The reiterated thud of the lead mallet seemed to give him satisfaction, for he continued hammering after the metal sheet was as flat as it would go. Presently he said, "Revolutions are bound to be harsh. You can't make that sort of omelet without breaking lives. And look! I do admit I'm in love with the girl herself. But if I was really *possessed* by the revolution, really fit to be a leader, I shouldn't love her that way. It's humiliating. I can't help being individualistically excited about her. I keep imagining all her body. Sometimes I wish I was on a South Sea island with her, alone with her, and living just for us two. Of course, I'm a sexual animal, and she's another; so my feeling that way about her is quite natural. But I ought to be able to rise above it all, for the revolution. I keep losing sight of the *realest* thing about her, just because of her hair and her eyes, and, well, the feel of her; and the way when we're together we seem to *belong* together, like a bolt and a nut. I mean, the *realest* thing about her is not really that sort of thing at all; it's just that she's a focal point where revolutionary forces in society find full expression. And the hell of it all is that if I give her up, as I once tried to do, I don't find it *easier* to concentrate on the revolution, but harder, much. I just think of nothing but her. Without her to watch me, my political work turns tiresome and silly." I laughed at him genially, but he did not respond.

We carried the repaired wing back to the car, and set about fixing it in position. I held it while he lay on his back to fit the bolts.

When the job was finished, he wriggled out from under the car, stood up, knocked the dust from his overalls, and said, dully, "The trouble with you comfortable people is always the same. You put up smoke screens to hide the truth from yourself, because you daren't face the consequences of seeing it. You talk about liberty (for the rich, of course) or personality, or the importance of expressing all sides of one's nature; and you won't see that today there's only one thing that is *really* important, namely that your class should be kicked out of its power and privileges. Everything else is just a sidetracking of historical forces that can't anyhow be halted but only delayed. And the longer they're delayed, the more misery. And now, look at the mess you have made of the world! Those of you who call yourselves socialists ought to be glad that socialism is established in one great country and is spreading over

Europe; but you don't welcome it; you're terrified lest people should insist on having it here. So you persuade yourselves it's not really socialism at all, and you spread all sorts of lies about it, and actually believe them yourselves. And now! You know your bloody system is falling to pieces, and the only way to bolster it up for a bit is to have war scares and actual wars. And now you have prostituted science by inventing an absolutely hellish weapon, and you're getting ready to smash Russia before it's too late, even if it means smashing the world. But Jesus Christ! We'll see you don't succeed."

Uncomfortably I admitted there was truth in what he had said, but insisted that it was only half the truth. I began to talk about the unreasonableness of Russian policy since the war. He broke in bitterly, "The West has played false every time, and now Russia's taking no more risks." I spoke of the unmistakable evidence of tyranny inside Russia. He protested, "It would be madness to be squeamish when the motherland is in danger. Besides! The capitalist press is plugging anti-Russian dope all the time."

He was wiping the smeared wing. "Well," he said, more amiably, "the job's finished. She looks pretty awful with that wing, but she'll travel safely. We had better just try her out on the road to test the steering." It was late in the afternoon. I said that I should need a meal before continuing my journey; and I suggested that we should take the car to some cafe and have a high tea together. "I can't do that," he said. "My time belongs to the boss till six o'clock." I replied that his time was *mine,* till the job was finished, and that was how I intended to finish it. I added that if he could make contact with his girl he could bring her, too. I also remarked that he would be doing no harm except to his employer, and employers were fair game. To my surprise he had scruples. "No!" he said. "He plays fair, and I will too. Honestly, I'd like to come, but it wouldn't be playing the game." I laughingly accused him of being still enslaved to bourgeois morality. Then I took the matter into my own hands, found the proprietor, told him I wanted to take his man away early and talk to him over a meal, and added that I would pay for his time off. The boss looked at me in amazement and said, "But you have both been arguing all day. Besides, I have work for him to do. If I am to run a concern like this I must stick to sound business principles, and not go soft to my employees." However, after I had pleaded with him and flattered him, his geniality triumphed over his principles. He said, "Oh, well! He's a useful lad, in fact a key man, and I can't afford to put him against me. I expected your job would take all day, and it hasn't, so my plans are not really upset any more than they were by letting you have him in the beginning. So take him, if you haven't had enough arguing even yet."

I paid my bill; and after the mechanic and I had cleaned ourselves up a bit, we set off in the car. He directed me from street to street, until at last we drew up in front of a drab little house. In a few moments he had found the girl and brought her to the car. As he introduced us, she showed signs of recognition, and I confessed that she had handed me a leaflet earlier in the day.

In the cafe, the two sat primly opposite me like children on their best behavior. They might have been at a children's party, waiting to be handed plates of trifle. They might have been brother and sister, for both had dark hair, deep eyes and a certain grace of movement, with which, I suspected, one had infected the other. I noticed that the girl's fastidious little nose had a slight downward curve, and that the wings of the nostrils were well marked. Her bright lips, flowerlike under the tip of her nose, were yet daintily compressed at the extremities. They at once invited and forbade. A chin like a small pale apricot lent firmness to the whole face.

I remarked to her that distributing leaflets was a job that always cowed me. However good the cause, I somehow hadn't the nerve to butt in on people. She flashed scorn at me, and said, "But surely it depends on the cause. If you don't really believe in it, of course you feel bad, even if you *think* you believe in it. But if you really, really believe in it, and especially if it is the most important of all causes, then you can't have any qualms at all. You would gladly *force* people to read your leaflets. You feel proud and glad to be on the job. And you don't notice when you're tired out." "And you are quite sure," I asked, "that your revolutionary propaganda is the most important of all causes?" "Naturally," she answered, with wide and earnest eyes. "What can possibly be more important than freeing the workers from exploitation by the rich, and founding the socialist world-state?"

Already, as you have guessed, knowing my weakness, I was half in love with this little fiery flower of a girl. But curiously I found myself less jealous of her lover than of the revolution.

I asked her if she was quite sure that the revolution really mattered so very much to her, more than personal values, like love and marriage and motherhood. She still gazed almost fiercely at me; but in the light of my earlier encounter with her I seemed to detect (or did I imagine?) a tremor in her eyes, slight as the quiver of a candle flame when a door is banged. She said, "Love matters to me very much, but the revolution matters very much more; because, you see, the revolution is going to make a world in which *all* loving can be far happier than it can ever be in our poisoning society. You see"—she glanced at her companion—"loving one person so much makes me love all others and want to help them. And so the revolution has got into my blood, into the very marrow that makes my blood."

All this while the young man was watching the face of his beloved with such tenderness that I was embarrassed. Perhaps he sensed my discomfort, for he suddenly compressed his lips, narrowed his eyes, and said gruffly, "The girl's right, you know. If the revolution really grips you, nothing else matters."

Still addressing the young woman, I said, "For the revolution, of course, you would not hesitate to lie and kill?" "Of course," she answered. "One mustn't be squeamish. Lying and killing are legitimate weapons for the revolution. They are wrong only when capitalists use them, *against* the revolution." I asked if she would even lie to her lover for the Revolution. "Of course, of course," she said. "I *might* have to lie to him. But he wouldn't really *be* my lover anymore if I had to lie to him for the revolution." She turned to her companion, and they looked at one another with grave affection.

The waitress arrived with our meal, and while she

arranged the table we kept silent. My lady guest, acting as hostess, poured out the tea. We all attacked our fish and chips.

Presently I challenged the girl again. I said, "Would you even *kill* the man you love, for the revolution? Probably you will say the need could not possibly arise, but people do sometimes lose their balance completely and turn against their own ideals. Or let us merely suppose that, though he remained loyal to the revolution, he had adopted a policy which you firmly believed to be disastrous. (Think of Trotsky and Stalin.) Suppose you were convinced that for the revolution his immediate destruction was necessary. (Oh, I know this is all crazy from your point of view, but just suppose.) Well, would you kill him?" Again the two looked gravely at each other. She put down her fork, and laid her hand on his wrist, and she said, "I don't know what I *would* do, but clearly I *ought* to kill him. It would be *right,* darling, wouldn't it? I mean, socially desirable." Her questioning smile was appealing and tender; but before he could answer, it changed into a look of excitement and fervor, and she declared, "Of course, of course I would kill him. To be true to the revolution, and also to be true to my own love for him, for the *real* him, who taught me so much, and helped me to give myself to the revolution, I should have to sacrifice him." They looked at each other in mutual adoration.

I munched my fish in silence.

Presently she wrenched her gaze from her dear victim; and then, seeing that our cups were empty, she took off the lid of the teapot, so that steam swelled from it as a tall column. She poured in hot water and filled our cups.

I said, "Another question, still more fantastic. You say that for the revolution you would lie and even kill. Would you, perhaps draw the line at torture? Or would you not? Let us suppose that someone fell into your power who possessed information vitally necessary for the revolution, and that he refused to surrender it. Would you use torture to extract it? Would you put him through the third degree? Would you go further and, well, tear off his fingernails one by one? Would you, for the revolution, gouge out his eyes?" Her brows knit and her deep eyes blazed, deliciously scourging me. She said, "Those are just silly abstract questions without any practical bearing." But I would not be put off. "They are nothing of the sort," I insisted. "They might become very practical questions. Don't funk the issue!"

After a silence, she laid down her knife and fork, and still looking at her plate, she said wearily, "Very well! Clearly I ought not to shrink even from torture, not if there was no other way of making the fascist beast give up his secret. Fascists themselves torture and sometimes we may be forced to pay them back in kind. But look! When fascists torture, it's just brutality. If ever *we* torture, it will be like a necessary surgical operation." Once more she looked at her companion. Once more that gaze of mutual comprehension. Once more, and more terrifyingly, her face was suddenly lit with ecstasy, and she said in a rapt voice, "Yes! Even if it was the man I had loved, I would tear off his nails one by one, and gouge out his eyes. I would do anything at all, to him or to myself, for the revolution." Her lover was now staring at her, fascinated, as though she was some terrible, lovely goddess.

A sluggish autumnal fly fell from the ceiling onto our table. It lay on its back, feebly kicking. All our eyes were directed to it. Then suddenly I was prompted by a malicious impulse to use this moribund creature as a means of shaking the girl's assurance. I took up a table knife and brought its cutting edge down on the fly's thorax, slowly pressing. Its struggles became suddenly violent, but soon they dwindled to a mere quiver, and then ceased. For a moment the girl watched its dying antics, her exaltation fading. Then, to my surprise and horror, she put her face in her hands, and a muffled sob escaped her. The young man laid his arm round her shoulder, but she shrugged him off. Lowering her hands, she flashed defiance at me. "That," she said, quietly, "was *not* necessary for the revolution."

I flicked away the corpse, and murmured shamefacedly, "Sorry! But it was only an insect, not a man; and noxious, in its little way."

The young man protested that I ought not to take a girl by surprise like that. Girls were more sensitive than men to the sight of suffering. All the more credit to those that forced themselves to overcome their squeamishness for the revolution. I apologized again; and felt distressfully that you, too, would have condemned me. The girl sat motionless, staring at the tablecloth.

To draw my attention from her, the young man embarked on a lecture. "Look!" he said, brushing back his unruly hair. "I think I can clear up our muddle. Of course there's nothing really *evil* about squashing flies, but some of us have been very heavily conditioned against hurting anything, and so we may be upset by it. Now, the taboo on cruelty has been socially justified. It is socially very important that people should dislike hurting anything, even an insect. We need a terrifically strong spirit of mutual kindliness among human beings, and we can well afford to have it so strong that the excess of it spills over onto animals. But very often, of course, we *have* to kill animals for the good of man. And it is quite irrational to be squeamish about it." Here I tried to interrupt, but he continued. "The same argument applies to killing and torturing human beings. When they turn antisocial, noxious to mankind, it's just social common sense to put them out of the way. And if they have valuable information and won't surrender it, surely it's common sense to get it out of them, even by torture, if necessary. We ought to overcome our squeamishness." I tried again to interrupt, but he said, "Wait a minute. Of course, to use torture lightheartedly, even on insects, is psychologically dangerous; and to use it on human beings is infinitely more so. It may undermine the established moral tradition, and so destroy mutual trust. It may break down the, well, the psychological warp on which society is woven. Believe me, I do see that. And it's important, though some of the comrades don't really see *how* important. The taboo against killing and torture, and the violent guilt feelings that decent people have about them, really are immensely important, just because they are socially useful. All the same, in an urgent revolutionary situation it's irrational, it's plain madness, to let our emotional habit of squeamishness endanger the revolution. I don't see how you can possibly answer this unless you claim there's some sort of *absolute* moral law that must never, never, in *any* circumstances, be broken. If you do claim this, then you will have to base your moral law on the will of God or some other fantastic notion."

While the young mechanic was delivering this lecture, the girl continued looking at the tablecloth. But when he had done, she touched his hand, and said, "Thank you for that. I knew I was right really; but I lost my balance. You saved me from my own squeamishness."

Unpleasantly I saw myself through the eyes of these two young enthusiasts as a pitiable but noxious creature, dominated unwittingly by fear of the revolution. Gloomily I wondered if they were right. I entertained this possibility, intellectually; but I *felt,* and with conviction, that these generous-hearted young people, through loyalty to the truth of Marx and Lenin, had blinded themselves to the deeper truth of Jesus, Buddha, Lao-tzu and all the saints.

How could I answer my friends' well-reasoned challenge? It seemed important that an answer should be made. It seemed to me at the time that the very integrity of the cosmos somehow depended on my answer, even though I knew intellectually that such a thought was farcical. Suddenly I was surprised by a ludicrous but startling fantasy. I felt that, crowding around us in that cramped little cafe, were all the great prophets and saints of every age and country, and even of worlds unknown to man; and they were commanding me to reveal the truth to this admirable though deluded boy and girl. I protested that for them, the believing saints, it was easy to answer from their belief; but for me difficult, from my unbelief. But they replied, "You in your unbelief have claimed, nevertheless, a certainty. Answer from your certainty."

Then, most irrationally, I prayed. I prayed in the hollow of my own heart, mutely. I prayed to the unknown for light.

At last I embarked on a halting affirmation such as you have heard from me a thousand times. And never yet have the words wrung wholly true, for either of us.

The young revolutionaries sat eating their apple tart in silence. Sometimes they watched me coldly, as a judge might scrutinize a prisoner who confutes himself unwittingly. But presently their eyes grew milder, not with credence, no, but at least with kindness.

I began by uneasily admitting that in some very rare circumstances even torture *might* perhaps be the right course. But I declared that, if social utility alone were taken as the sole criterion of good and evil, torture and every kind of harshness would be far too tempting to those who, whether as rulers or rebels, believed themselves to be custodians of social utility. Little by little, but inevitably, society would be brutalized through and through. "That way," I said, "lies the degradation of man to insect." I declared, with a conviction that surprised even myself, that the taboo against torture must be felt to spring

from something truly sacred. (Here the girl grim-
aced, the man sighed.) This something more than
man, I freely granted, must not be thought of as a
personal God, nor even as some principle fundamental to the cosmos; for such things, I insisted, were
utterly beyond the reach of our understanding. As
well might a worm explain humanity as a man
expound the foundations of the cosmos. At this the
young man nodded cautious approval.

Then, uncertainly, I bore witness to my certainty.
I said my piece that you have heard so often, my
piece about the spirit. Familiar as it is to you (oh, too
familiar), I find I must now say it all over again,
because under the scrutiny of those young earnest
eyes I found myself phrasing it in a subtly different
idiom or with a new accent.

"This something," I said, "this all-important thing,
is at once *in* us, and yet not just *ourselves*. It is
something in a way distinct from us that we see
inwardly. It is something in relation to which (when
we really, really see it) the whole human species
seems not an end but a means; an instrument for
realizing this something, this glorious possibility.
Oneself, and others, and the whole species come to
seem unimportant save insofar as they succeed in
embodying or expressing this possibility, this ideal,
this, yes, this spirit, in concrete human living. And
yet, if we are honest, we are forced to recognize that
the human mind cannot possibly understand what
the status of this thing is, in the universe as a whole.
We know it only in ourselves and each other, and in
our loving each other; and of course in all the forms
of our conscious and creative behavior. But love is

the very tissue of it. The tissue, I mean, of the vision that we have of it. For it confronts us as a vision. What *gives* us the vision we cannot know. It is a vision that simply emerges out of the relation between a conscious being and an objective universe containing other conscious beings. So this 'something,' this spirit, presents itself as a vision of a *way of behaving* in relation to the objective universe; an ideal way of life. It is the way of sensitive and intelligent awareness of everything that comes up against one in the business of living. It is the way of love for all lovely things; and of at least sympathetic understanding for all unlovely things; yes, and even of love for them in an odd sort of style. But above all it is the way of creative action in relation to the real world of minds and things; action not just for action's sake, or to make a big noise or a big mark on the universe, but action to make more loveliness and more loving, I mean more sensitive and intelligent loving; in fact, it is essentially the way of action to fulfill and express the, well, the spiritual potentiality of—of?—well, of the objective universe itself in its impact on subjective beings."

I paused to think of the next thing to say. The eyes of the couple were upon me, interested, a little troubled, fundamentally aloof. "Go on!" the young man said.

This ideal," I declared, "this spirit, has gradually revealed itself throughout the ages to the most sensitive human minds. And we ourselves, in our clearest state, cannot but recognize its claims on us. Moreover, though we know so little about the universe, we can be quite sure (in virtue of our experience of spirit) that all personal beings throughout the whole cosmos of space and time must joyfully worship this thing, whenever they are properly awake and not misled by obsessions over trivial irrelevant cravings. And this vision of the spirit, this recognition of 'fittingness,' 'appropriateness,' in personal behavior, is the true sanction of right and wrong. Killing and torture are in themselves always evil just because they are a flagrant violation of the spirit. No doubt, in our sick-adolescent world, killing is sometimes necessary (and many other evils, too), but only in defense of the spirit. And only those who have a deep and *spiritual* loathing of killing (not a mere sickly squeamishness) are to be trusted to kill (or sanction killing) *only* when loyalty to the spirit itself demands it. And it is the same with torture, but with a difference; for even in our barbaric society we can be sure that in practice there are *no* situations in which it is justified. For *no* immediate goal can compensate for the hideous degradation that it causes, in the torturer and in society."

I could say no more. The cloud of unseen witnesses that had seemed to press in upon me faded from the room, withdrawing (it seemed to me) with a sigh, whether of fulfillment or of disappointment I could not determine.

The three of us sat in silence. Then the young man said, sadly, "Ideas like those have power, but it is a hypnotic power, appealing to the infantile need for something great and imposing, like the father, and later the leader. Be careful, comrade, lest you trick yourself into some sort of fascism. Because, you know, fascists can support their brutal values by arguments like yours, based on *feeling* instead of intelligence."

I answered desperately, "They can, of course, but falsely. Their values are opposed fundamentally to the whole great spiritual tradition of mankind; and also to our own individual intuition when we are most clearly conscious, most fully ourselves, not distracted by some irrelevant craving, like the craving for power. And think! In personal relations most of us know quite well the difference between two kinds of relation that are both called love, but one of them quite falsely. We know the difference between using a girl as a mere means to one's own satisfaction, and really loving her." The two glanced at each other. I continued. "Of course, if you have never really loved you cannot know what that difference is. And in the same way, if you have never really experienced the spirit you cannot possibly see the difference between it and the counterfeit of it that Marxism and Freudianism so glibly explain."

Suddenly I noted that my guests were already smoking, and that a cigarette had been put down for me on the table. The young man was expelling from his lungs a great cloud of smoke. He dispersed it with his hand, as though brushing aside my fog of words. He said, "Well, at least you have made me see how seductive the old ideas can be, especially if one *needs* a smoke screen." Suddenly, the wink once more violently assailed him; and he said, surprisingly, "Something deep down in me makes me wish you were right. If I didn't wish it so much, I shouldn't need to be so much on my guard." The girl, who had been dreamily watching me, turned to her lover with a sudden look of perplexity.

Then again she gazed at me, holding her lip-stained cigarette in a poised hand, while from her nostrils smoke wreaths caressed her face. Still studying me, she murmured to him, "He really believes it." Then after a draught of smoke, she said, "He's earnest about it. Suppose he really has got hold of some truth he can't properly tell. In a way I can sort of feel it." But in a harder voice she declared, "But today it's not what we need. It's an irrelevance and dangerous. Gentleness, and all that, is dangerous. We must keep it locked tight in our hearts. We must be made of steel. For today, the struggle."

Evidently this amazon had tasted poetry, at least the modern poetry of the revolution.

"Comrade," she said, and she could not prevent the imprisoned gentleness from looking out from her eyes, "I shall be sorry if in the end we have to liquidate you." She smiled. It was the smile that I had intruded upon when first we met. I duly laughed.

Turning to her lover, she hauled up his watch from his breast pocket, and glancing at it she cried, "Half-past already! And we have to arrange the hall for the meeting."

The two rose hurriedly, and I secured my bill. As we shook hands for parting, the mechanic said quietly, "I'm glad you had that breakdown."